Nonviolence:
Origins & Outcomes

Second Edition

Charles E. Collyer
&
Ira G. Zepp, Jr.

Foreword by
Bernard LaFayette, Jr.

Published by
TRAFFORD
USA • Canada • UK • Ireland

Second Edition

First edition published in 2003 by Writers Workshop.

Note for Librarians: A cataloguing record for this book is available from Library and
Archives Canada at www.collectionscanada.ca/amicus/index-e.html
ISBN 1-4251-0425-8

PUBLISHING™
Offices in Canada, USA, Ireland and UK

Book sales for North America and international:
Trafford Publishing, 6E–2333 Government St.,
Victoria, BC V8T 4P4 CANADA
phone 250 383 6864 (toll-free 1 888 232 4444)
fax 250 383 6804; email to orders@trafford.com
Book sales in Europe:
Trafford Publishing (UK) Limited, 9 Park End Street, 2nd Floor
Oxford, UK OX1 1HH UNITED KINGDOM
phone 44 (0)1865 722 113 (local rate 0845 230 9601)
facsimile 44 (0)1865 722 868; info.uk@trafford.com
Order online at:
trafford.com/06-2182

10 9 8 7 6 5 4 3 2

Biographical Sketches

Charles E. Collyer

Charles Collyer, a native of Hamilton, Canada, received his doctorate in Psychology from Princeton University in 1976. He is Professor of Psychology, and a former Chair of his department, at the University of Rhode Island. He was a co-founder of the Center for Nonviolence and Peace Studies at URI. He lives in Providence, Rhode Island and in Westminster, Maryland, where, with Dr. Pamela Zappardino, he also co-directs the Ira and Mary Zepp Center for Nonviolence and Peace Education.

Ira G. Zepp, Jr.

Ira Zepp received his doctorate from St. Mary's Seminary and University, and did graduate work in Islam at Hartford Theological Seminary. He has studied in India, Mexico, Israel, and Eastern Europe. For 31 years he taught religious studies at McDaniel College (formerly Western Maryland College). He is the author of many articles and eight books, two of which are related to the thought of Martin Luther King, Jr. Presently, he is Professor Emeritus of Religious Studies at McDaniel College.

Bernard LaFayette, Jr.

Bernard LaFayette, the author of the Foreword, was a member of Martin Luther King's executive staff during the U.S. Civil Rights Movement, and has been a nonviolence educator for over forty years. A Harvard University Ed.D., he is a former President of his alma mater, American Baptist College in Nashville, Tennessee. He currently chairs the International Nonviolence Conference Board, and is Distinguished Scholar-in-Residence and Director of the Center for Nonviolence and Peace Studies at the University of Rhode Island.

Toward a Positive Future

I believe that the sum total of the energy of mankind is not to bring us down but to lift us up, and that is the result of the definite, if unconscious, working of the law of love. The fact that mankind persists shows that the cohesive force is greater than the disruptive force. You must never despair of human nature.

Mohandas K. Gandhi

The way of acquiescence leads to moral and spiritual suicide. The way of violence leads to bitterness in the survivors and brutality in the destroyers. But the way of nonviolence leads to redemption and the creation of the beloved community.

Martin Luther King, Jr.

Dedications

For John Lidgey, 1948-2001, my friend of 50 years,
who was intensely interested in this project.
In grateful memory.
- Charlie.

&

For Montgomery J. Shroyer – Biblical scholar, social
activist, nonviolence teacher.
With gratitude and respect.
- Ira.

Contents

Preface

We are grateful to the many students and friends – old and new – who enjoyed the limited first edition of *Nonviolence: Origins and Outcomes*, published in 2003 by our colleague Dr. P. Lal of the Writers Workshop in Kolkata, India.

In this second edition some minor revisions and corrections have been made. Some lines of thought have been clarified, and some references to current events have been updated. The book will be quite recognizable to those who already know it. With the help of Trafford Publishing, we look forward to making the book more widely available to new audiences.

The main message remains: There is more to learn about nonviolence than we thought when we began to study it. If you too find this to be true, after delving into the topic, you will find yourself to be in the company of many good folks.

The principal task for those of us interested in nonviolence education seems to be cracking open the outwardly uninspiring term *nonviolence* to reveal the wealth of stories, ideas, values, applications, personalities, skills, and approaches to problem solving from all over the world that this term signifies, but also conceals.

We have tried to introduce the richness of nonviolence, ranging from its traditional origins to its observable outcomes and potential applications in peoples' lives today. This is not a detailed text, but an invitation to participate in a learning process. We hope that you will enjoy it.

Foreword

The past century has brought humankind into an era of mass destruction, one where our ability to produce massive suffering has raced ahead of our capacity to demonstrate compassion for one another.

We must search for paths into a 21st century that will turn away from destructive goals and strategies, that will reject violence as a way to solve problems. If we are to rise to a new level, it will be necessary for us to re-examine basic concepts, re-draw our roadmap, re-direct our footsteps, and re-shape our vision for the future.

This book by Charles Collyer and Ira Zepp makes a significant contribution to the field of nonviolence and peace studies. The experience of the authors as teachers of nonviolence and the depth of their commitment to nonviolent social change, is evident in every chapter. Many scholars and practitioners will benefit greatly from this work, particularly those who have recently come into this field of study and are developing their own skills as teachers of peace. This book lays out a foundation of ahimsa, love, and achievable nonviolence, which belongs in the forefront of the new century's search for a new way.

Dr. Bernard LaFayette, Jr.

Prologue

Charles E. Collyer

It was mid-January, the beginning of a Spring semester at the University of Rhode Island. I was the instructor for a group of first-year graduate students in Psychology in the department's orientation seminar. The people in this class were impressive. All had come to the university with strong credentials. They displayed an obvious enthusiasm for learning more about the field, and had high expectations of their program faculty. Most were in their mid-twenties to mid-thirties, some coming directly from bachelor's degree programs and some from the working world. They were not kids, but grown men and women with at least a semester of graduate work under their belts, already well educated and pretty sophisticated.

In this particular seminar, about twenty students from three doctoral tracks - clinical, experimental, and school psychology - were all mixed together. This integration was more the exception than the rule in their courses, because for the most part the three programs functioned separately. In this seminar, however, the students were getting to know each other during their first year, and learning about the department's faculty, its research resources, and the current state of the field of psychology.

We were meeting on a Monday. The Martin Luther King Jr. holiday was coming up the following week, so our second seminar meeting of the new semester would be in two weeks time, and I made an announcement to that effect. Then, having mentioned the holiday, I happened to ask how many people had ever read King's *Letter from Birmingham Jail*. No one raised a hand.

I had become a nonviolence trainer about two years before. In that role, I had often assigned the *Letter from Birmingham Jail* and led discussions on it. But my nonviolence workshops had usually consisted of younger students or members of community groups. I had never assigned King to graduate students in Psychology.

I was surprised that no one in this well-educated group had read the *Letter*. I asked how many people had ever read anything by Martin Luther King. Only a couple of hands were raised. One person related that when she had been in high school, her class had spent a day learning about the Civil Rights Movement. She knew Dr. King mainly for the "I Have a Dream" speech, which she remembered reading. She was hazy on the details of what had happened during the Movement. She had heard that I was involved in nonviolence training, and that the curriculum I used was derived from King and Gandhi. She remembered thinking recently that her brief high school exposure to the Civil Rights Movement had not included a discussion of nonviolence, or King's relationship to it.

I decided that this was obviously one of those "teachable moments," when a gap has been acknowledged and the next step would be to fill it in. I said something like this: "Well, I'm going to give you an assignment. Go out and find something to read by Dr. King. It can be the *Letter from Birmingham Jail*, or anything else. When we get back together in two weeks we can talk about what you found. I'm especially interested in what you think about King as a psychologist." I left open the question whether 'as a psychologist' meant 'the psychologist', placing King in the role, or 'from a psychological viewpoint,' inviting the student to be the psychologist. As a result, some people interpreted the assignment one way, and some the other way.

This was probably the most successful homework assignment I have ever given to a group of students, at any level. When the group met again two weeks later, they were genuinely excited about King and nonviolence and civil rights and the psychology of it all. They had obtained King's *Letter*, and other books, sermons, and essays. Several expressed amazement that they had not known of King as a thinker and writer before this. Some had decided to participate in one of the King Holiday events because of the assignment. The students were full of admiration for King's moral approach to difficult conflicts, for his ability to respect and even care for his adversaries, for his skill as a coalition-builder. And they were fascinated by the dynamics of nonviolence, by its counterintuitive yet very natural quality, and by its power at times to cut through human problems and provide surprising solutions. The relevance of nonviolence for psychology, and vice versa, just leapt out at them. One student asked, quite early in our discussion, "Why didn't I ever have a course on this?" Indeed.

On that day I began to wonder why psychology and the traditions of nonviolence were not in closer touch with each other. Because the historical origins of nonviolence lay outside the relatively young field of psychology, in other disciplines and in nonacademic arenas, it was understandable that the topic had not made its way into the standard curricula of our degree programs. But the impact of nonviolence in practice, and its influence on people's thinking and emotions, loudly say "psychology" to me, and I have come to believe that a stronger bridge needs to be built between the two domains.

Nonviolence grew originally from religious roots. Psychology is a secular, not a religious, field of study. Yet many psychologists readily acknowledge that some "spiritual" understanding of life is important to them, and that though they find spirituality largely missing from the mainstream of their field, they feel it is an important element in their own work and in understanding human nature. Martin Luther

King Jr., and Mahatma Gandhi before him, each crafted a practical social vision of his religion, combining a positive, spiritually satisfying view of humankind with political energy for progress toward freedom and justice. Psychologists join with many other audiences in finding that this combination of spirituality and practicality fills a void for them.

This book is written to whet an appetite for nonviolence, in as many readers as possible. We think it will appeal especially to the many students of psychology, and people interested in psychology, who also have an interest in spiritual and social values. More generally, we believe that nonviolence offers "common ground" where religious and secular concerns can intersect, and where bridges can be built between cultures, disciplines, and factions of many kinds. We have seen the study and practice of nonviolence reap rich rewards, and so wish to encourage as many people as possible to explore this common ground and try out the building and crossing of these bridges.

Where We are Coming From

As authors, we bring different kinds of training to this book, but we share an interest in how people can apply nonviolence to everyday life. Indeed, it was this interest in how to make ideals practical that brought us together. Ira Zepp brings a religious and philosophical orientation to this task. An early student of Martin Luther King Jr.'s intellectual roots, he has participated in many nonviolent actions for social change over the past five decades. As a teacher at McDaniel College (formerly Western Maryland College), he has introduced hundreds of students to nonviolence through courses on Gandhi and King. He is Professor Emeritus of Religious Studies at McDaniel, and was Dean of the Chapel there from 1963 to 1978.

Charles Collyer brings a psychological orientation to the book. A Professor of Psychology at the University of Rhode Island, he helped to found the Center for Nonviolence and Peace Studies there. He has both developed courses on nonviolence and carried out nonviolence training with many groups and organizations in the community. With Dr. Pamela Zappardino, he also co-founded the Ira and Mary Zepp Center for Nonviolence and Peace Education, a program of Common Ground on the Hill[1], in Westminster, Maryland. He thanks Dr. Zappardino for her advice and editorial help in the preparation of this book.

The authors acknowledge that many fields of knowledge in addition to philosophy, religious studies, and psychology, contribute to nonviolence. We feel that nonviolence probably deserves to be a major field of knowledge in its own right. But instead, its content is distributed widely among several disciplines that history has decreed are the official ones to be taught in schools and colleges. Nonviolence is certainly embraced as an important topic of study in the emerging field of peace and conflict studies.[2] In writing this book, we have tried to adopt an interdisciplinary, inclusive attitude, without pretending to be very sophisticated about sociology, communication studies, political science, international relations, women's studies, or any of the many other areas which also own pieces of this "big tent". We ask our colleagues' pardon for the inadequacies of our coverage in their diverse areas.

Notes

1. *Common Ground on the Hill* is an organization using the traditional music and arts of different groups of people to create opportunities for dialogue and greater mutual understanding.   Each summer, Common Ground holds "traditions weeks" consisting of courses in musical, artistic, and social traditions, as well as concerts and other performances. For more information about these programs, see the web site www.commongroundonthehill.org.

2. See, for example, this readable text: Barash, D. P. & Webel, C. P. (2002). *Peace and Conflict Studies*. Thousand Oaks CA: Sage Publications.

Chapter i

Discovering Nonviolence

Charles E. Collyer

Nonviolence is not just another topic. Learning about nonviolence has ended up being a life-transforming experience for many people all over the world, offering a new way to look at life and how to solve its problems, and opening up unexpected opportunities for change. Is this claim surprising to you? It was to me. After I became convinced that it was really true, I became curious about exactly why "nonviolence" came as this profound revelation to so many of the people who studied it.

Before they dig into the stories and the conceptual richness of nonviolence, most potential students of the topic seem to have a stereotype about it - a set of beliefs that, by default, captures the meaning of the word "nonviolence" for them. First, they probably think of nonviolence as a *passive* philosophical approach in which things are just allowed to happen without any intervention or interference. Second, they may associate nonviolence with *cowardice*, and violence with courage. Third, they may equate nonviolence with just *being nice* to people. And fourth, they may see nonviolence as being *easy*, as the path of least resistance in many of life's challenging situations.

A little study soon shows that nonviolence is the very opposite in every respect. It involves active problem solving rather than passive acquiescence. It very often requires awesome courage in the face of real threats and terrible fear. It is likely to demand difficult confrontations, and intense discomfort both for the just and the unjust. And it has therefore been the more difficult path, the road less traveled, in almost all of its most famous examples. These contrasts, and others, help to explain why the discovery of nonviolence very often involves a series of surprises for the new student.

So why does the old stereotype of nonviolence exist, and persist? Many reasons could be given, but it seems to us that the understanding of nonviolence as passive, cowardly, "nice", and easy, is maintained by very strong psychological and cultural forces, some of which are paradoxical and hard to perceive, much less to challenge. We will discuss some of these forces in this chapter and throughout the book.

Despite these forces, nonviolence continues to be rediscovered by people who need it. Throughout history, in many cultures all over the world, people have discovered the power of nonviolent motives, feelings, tactics, and values. Nonviolence has given direction to religions, enabled embattled peoples to survive, and achieved dramatic triumphs over injustice and violence.[1] However, the understanding of nonviolence as a powerful antidote to both violence and complacency is also often lost, or submerged in a culture's repertoire of traditions, and so must be explicitly rediscovered again in response to a new set of problems.

Between rediscoveries, when people have slid into acceptance and even glorification of violence, and when wealth and distance enable many people to evade basic human problems rather than solve them, the stereotyped view of nonviolence – passive, cowardly, nice, easy – prevails. The stereotype is abetted by the structure of the word itself: "nonviolence" sounds like it should simply mean "not violent", with apparently obvious negative and passive connotations.

Possessing this understanding of nonviolence, people paradoxically both approve of nonviolence, and are frightened and confused by it. They endorse it as a remedy for the violence that frightens or annoys them, and are enthusiastic about its adoption by others. However, they confidently "know" that they themselves could not stick with nonviolence if their own lives or family were threatened. They proclaim that nonviolence will not work in situations that have reached crisis proportions.

Well, to address the last point first, sometimes nonviolence has worked in crisis situations. But for some reason we do not tell stories about the courageous and successful use of nonviolence very often. Perhaps nonviolence is just as frightening to us as violence! Perhaps we believe that we will be rendered vulnerable if we embrace nonviolence, as if we were not already so. Perhaps we refrain from telling stories about nonviolence, so as to protect ourselves, and our loved ones, from exposure to danger.

But what if those stories were more likely to help us survive than to put us in danger? It would then be tragic if we did not tell them and try to learn from them. We will tell some of the stories of nonviolence in this book, and you can judge their value for yourself. Some of the stories are indeed about crisis situations, but many are about how crises can be prevented, and problems solved, through the way in which lives are lived.

Here are two analogies that seem to capture the idea of nonviolence as a life-long practice or skill rather than a passing decision or temporary tactic:

First, quitting smoking is never seriously suggested as a cure for the person who is already dying of lung cancer. Rather, we understand that quitting, done early enough, can reduce a person's risk of getting lung cancer in the first place. We would not test the value of "quitting smoking" by its failure to cure a terminally ill person. Yet nonviolence is often put to such a test, as a form of eleventh-hour crisis intervention. Nonviolence is often deemed to have failed when, in a crisis, it does not magically make the threat of violence go away. This is unfair; it is like dismissing the value of quitting smoking after the critically ill quitter dies anyway. Why would people reject nonviolence unfairly? Perhaps this is one of the ways in which we human beings defend ourselves against the supposed dangers of adopting nonviolence. "See? We tried nonviolence, and it didn't work." (That is, it didn't magically overcome violence right now.) "Now, let's go back to our old habits."

A second meaningful comparison is to swimming. Learning nonviolence is very much like learning to swim. Like swimming, nonviolence is enriching, useful in everyday tasks, preventive of threats to life, and very helpful when threats nevertheless arise. Everyone understands the value of swimming lessons. Well, there are nonviolence lessons, too. In the U.S. Civil Rights Movement and in other human rights movements around the world, nonviolence training was, and still is, undertaken to prepare for predictable threats to life and limb such as being beaten up or attacked by police dogs. Demonstrators in the campaigns where nonviolence was the guiding principle were not thrown unprepared into the sea of injustice and hostility, but received lessons ahead of time that taught them what to expect and how to respond.

"Sink or swim" is a phrase referring to the limited, frightening options of an unprepared person floundering in crisis. Sometimes this phrase is actually adopted as a strategy for learning how to swim, in which case it means plunging the student into a crisis on the first day of the course. We leave to others the task of interpreting the merits and shortcomings of this approach. But regardless of how one was introduced to the water, it is clearly best to take lessons, get lots of practice, and master the skills of swimming well before a real crisis arises when floundering simply will not do. And the same might be said for many other skills, including the skills of nonviolence.

If we are lucky, crises occupy only a fraction of our lives.

Nonviolence may or may not provide the solution during the 1% (say) of our days when we are in real crisis. But it certainly provides valuable guidance during the other 99%. In fact, it might be said that all the problems successfully solved, and then often forgotten, that occupy this larger portion of our time, are examples of nonviolence at work. Should we not study our own successes in order to learn how to have more of them? In this book, we will present nonviolence as something to practice not just when the threat of violence is about to overwhelm us, but all of the time. We believe that this approach is in keeping with what Mahatma Gandhi and Martin Luther King, Jr. meant by nonviolence.

So, What Does Nonviolence Mean?

We have said that the old stereotype of nonviolence is mistaken, and we have said that the structure of the word itself gives a wrong impression of what nonviolence means. We have said that nonviolence is not just a way of responding to crisis, but an approach applicable to the whole of life. We have also suggested that successful problem solving can be regarded as nonviolence. Before we go further, we should try to say just what nonviolence means to us.

Sure enough, nonviolence means being opposed to violence. One of the origins of nonviolence presented in Part I of this book is *ahimsa*, the Sanskrit word meaning non-injury. But nonviolence also means valuing and caring about human beings, simply because they are people; accordingly, the other root of nonviolence is *agape*, the Greek word for unconditional love toward others. In addition to these two roots, the meaning of nonviolence also resides in the lives of people who are trying to follow a nonviolent path. These outcomes are the focus of Part II of this book. So for us nonviolence also has come to mean a collection of outcomes that go beyond opposition to violence: a goal-oriented approach to life, a fearlessly realistic way of facing problems, and a wide variety of forms of personal investment and commitment.

As you can see, nonviolence for us is a many-faceted idea, or perhaps a constellation of many ideas. Throughout history, many versions of nonviolence have developed, some from religious traditions and some with more secular or combined roots. We adopt an inclusive, "big tent" approach, in which all of these versions are valued, and are seen as tending in the same general direction. We do not presume to speak for them all, but we will try to refrain from elevating one specific version over another. Can a general, "big tent" definition of nonviolence be given? Perhaps not to everyone's satisfaction, given this complicated picture, but here is an attempt:

Nonviolence is an approach to life in which people are valued for their own sake, and in which the idea of successful living includes peace achieved through peaceful means. It demands the best that people have to offer, both in crisis situations and in the course of everyday life. It is active, courageous, realistic, and challenging. It can be learned. Nonviolence does not have to be performed perfectly. But to the extent that it can be practiced, it makes a valuable contribution to the quality of life and to relationships between people, whether they are friends or adversaries, by creating conditions that support human beings rather than doing violence to them.

OBSTACLES AND PARADOXES

We hope we have made nonviolence sound interesting and attractive – a "good deal" - so far. It has been so attractive to some of our students that they have asked us for advice on how to make a career out of teaching nonviolence! A few of them have actually done it. It turns out, however, that advocating for nonviolence on a large scale is quite difficult. For many people in society, significant obstacles stand in the way of adopting nonviolence. Some of the problems are paradoxical and even funny, at least up to a point. In our opinion, there is a pressing need for more understanding of these problems of nonviolence education and for more people who are willing to work on overcoming them. Here are just a few of the obstacles we have encountered in our work:

First, everyone in the world seems to believe that the world would be better off if only *everyone else* were less violent. Now, if everyone endorses nonviolence at least to this extent, why is the world still so violent? Clearly, we need to come to terms, not only with other people's violence, but also with our own. Ironically, most of us have a strong, even desperate, tendency to cling to violence as an option for ourselves, and to avoid serious consideration of living without this option.

Second, the wisdom of the ages, regarding violence and the feelings associated with it, is sometimes not so wise. For example, the idea that anger must be cathartically "vented" is very widespread; in fact, many people believe that, when angry, greater harm will come to them if they take some time to think about how to respond than if they act out their anger immediately. But fifty years of research, less widely known, supports the alternative view that (1) the perceived necessity of venting anger is a compelling illusion, and (2) learning skills to deal with anger is more effective in almost every way.[2]

Third, when the wisdom of the ages really is wise, we sometimes just don't get it. An example is the Golden Rule: *Treat others as you want them to treat you.* For the most part, this is a profoundly good, nonviolent insight.[3] It is proactive, giving a guideline for our behavior for us to apply in advance of knowing what others' behavior will be. Too often, however, we operate on what might be called the Rule of Payback: *Treat others the way they have treated you* (also expressed in the

familiar equation: An eye for an eye and a tooth for a tooth.)
Some people apparently cannot distinguish between these two
rules; they just don't get the difference. Justice is equated,
not with fair and respectful treatment for all, but with getting
revenge; and peace is equated, not with positive, constructive
lives and relationships, but simply with being left alone.

Fourth, we human beings become adapted to unjust and
destructive conditions all too readily. What is *familiar* to us
through long experience – even if it is ghastly - comes to feel
normal through mere exposure and repetition. And violence
is usually repetitive. Most of the violence in the world occurs
in repeated cycles of payback for the most recent outrage of
our enemies, which in turn was justified by them as a response
to our own attacks, and so on and so on. With a moment's
reflection, it is clear that a great deal of the world's violence
could be prevented if people could stop these cycles. But we
are accustomed to these cycles, precisely because the pattern is
repetitive. We tell ourselves that this is normal, natural, the way
things have always been. Some even object to nonviolence as
abnormal and unnatural, probably because they are unfamiliar
with its richer meaning.

Fifth, although violence and hostility are real threats to
everyone, we do not often teach the ideas and methods of
nonviolence. We could do so; the knowledge is available. In
fact, a lot of it will be introduced in this book. But to propose
that nonviolence be taught in schools is very controversial in
many communities. In some places the objection is that it
is not an academic subject. In others it is greeted with the
suspicion that it is religion or that it is politically slanted.
Other communities will claim that they do not need it, even
as bullying goes on in school hallways, teenage drivers (in
imitation of their elders) succumb to road rage, and badly
handled emotions lead to partner abuse and rape.

This list could be extended, but already it provides a glimpse of what could be called resistance to nonviolence: a complex of obstacles and paradoxical elements in human life, which prevent us from taking greater advantage of nonviolence to live more successfully.

WELCOMED NONETHELESS

Resistance to nonviolence is based on some real fears and concerns, which teachers of nonviolence should acknowledge. When people's feelings and needs are respected, the richer and more inclusive version of nonviolence that we are talking about in this book will be welcomed by most audiences.

Nonviolence is perhaps most warmly welcomed in communities where violence is most overt and prevalent. Although people may carry the old stereotype of nonviolence with them when they come in for a workshop or other presentation, and although their initial response may be slightly cynical or suspicious, audiences usually recognize quickly that "this nonviolence stuff" is important knowledge to possess. A teacher often senses that there is a widespread hunger out there for the ideas and skills of nonviolence, a hunger which most schools and other institutions apparently do little to alleviate.

LEVELS: FROM INDIVIDUAL TO INTERNATIONAL

As a working hypothesis, we will claim that the basic ideas of nonviolence are applicable from the individual and interpersonal levels, up to the societal and global levels of human life and problem solving.

For example, every intentional act of violence, from the individual to the international, seems to have a compelling rationale in the mind of at least one human being. One man was only trying to teach his wife a lesson. Another had no choice – the other guy at the bar had given him "the look." A young woman felt justified in slapping her child, because the kid just wouldn't shut up, even after she had yelled at him. A gang carried out a "hit" on a rival gang member pre-emptively, because he was expected to lead an attack against them. A general ordered his troops to destroy a village in retaliation for a sniper attack, and called in air support to eliminate an enemy gun position. In a talk on just-war theory, a national security advisor attempted to summarize the conditions under which it is rational and proper to wage war. This advisor had given similar speeches about three recent wars, arguing that in each case the conditions for a just war had been satisfied.

Are there similar dynamics of felt necessity and justification at work in these cases? We suspect the answer is yes. Cognitive and emotional psychology is quite relevant to understanding what is going on before, during, and after violence.[4] If we learn that a person committed an act of violence, we can be fairly sure that the person perceived (correctly or mistakenly) that they had been threatened, disrespected, or harmed by somebody else. Or they may have been afraid that they were about to lose power and control over another person, such as a spouse or partner. There was almost certainly a personal logic on the part of the violent actor, which rationalized his or her (it is usually his) violence. James Gilligan has argued that almost all violence involves feeling shamed or disrespected, and believing that one is acting out of self-defense, self-protection, or justifiable self-assertion.[5]

Another aspect of violence that seems to run the gamut of levels, from personal conflicts to wars, is a tendency by the agents of violence to discount the "collateral damage" caused by their behavior. Violence causes both intentional effects (harm done that the violent actor meant to cause) and incidental effects (harm done that was not intended). Collateral damage is a euphemism for the incidental destruction of violence, but the labels "collateral" and "incidental" are meaningless to the people who are harmed. Effects are effects. There is no law of nature saying that the intended effects of violence will be the only significant ones, the most lasting, the most remembered, or the only ones for which the initiators of the violence will be held responsible for. In fact, damage that one party regards as "collateral" may very well become the reason in another's mind for the next round of retaliation.

The subjectivity and arbitrariness of what is called collateral damage are greatly under-appreciated by violent people. The main thing on a violent person's mind at the time of the violence is a highly personal fantasy about control, revenge, punishment, or destruction. The imagined consequences of the violence make up a distorted cartoon: that the enemy or other object of attack will be eliminated or neutralized, and that the problem of the moment will therefore be solved. It never turns out to be as surgically effective in reality as it was in the violent person's mind; there are always messy collateral consequences, which are every bit as real as any intentional damage that is "accomplished." But at the time of the violence, these downstream consequences are conveniently minimized in the mind of the violent actor. One of the factors that undermines the credibility of "just war" claims is that the cost-benefit calculation, which ostensibly precedes a decision to wage war, is inevitably rigged by this discounting of the costs of collateral damage.[6]

We are claiming that nonviolence has important things to say about these and other problems, which range from individual problem-solving to the global level. We do acknowledge that the difficulties in applying nonviolence are significant, and daunting. However, one advantage of adopting a broadly inclusive vision of nonviolence is that the full range of human creativity and potential for constructive problem solving can be brought to bear.

OVERVIEW OF THE BOOK

The title of this book, *Nonviolence: Origins and Outcomes*, is a miniature outline. Part I is about Origins. More specifically, it is about *agape* and *ahimsa*, which we regard as the two principal roots of nonviolence. These concepts grow out of Christian, Hindu, and related religious traditions. Ira Zepp identifies several sources in these traditions that speak most directly to nonviolence, and develops topics such as the manifestation of *agape* through forgiveness, and the balancing of ideals with practicality in everyday life. He calls attention to "approximations" of *agape* and *ahimsa,* which deserve our attention if we are to appreciate the potential for application of nonviolence in real situations.

Part II is about Outcomes, by which we mean the kinds of transformation and change that occur as people discover and learn about nonviolence. There is a sampling of initial reactions to examples of nonviolence from some of Charles Collyer's students. A powerfully effective version of nonviolence training is described, as are some of the aspects of nonviolence that seem especially salient for people who have gone through this type of training. A dialogue between Ira Zepp and Bill Holmes about the September 11, 2001 attacks, is offered as a window into the "big tent" containing both people who identify with nonviolence (such as Ira), and people who are sympathetic critics of nonviolence (such as Bill). Finally, two issues related to the practicality of nonviolence – measurable outcomes and nonviolent responses to threat - are confronted and discussed.

If you are new to nonviolence, we hope this book will open up the topic for you, and leave you eager to learn more. If you are already familiar with one or more of the traditions of nonviolence, we hope that our combination of ideas will provide a valuable new slant on this fascinating, vitally important, and inherently interdisciplinary and multicultural field of study.

Notes

1. For examples, see *A Force More Powerful* , the Public Broadcasting System series of six short documentaries on successful nonviolent movements for social and political change in India, the United States, Poland, South Africa, Chile, and Denmark. The book of the same name contains chapters on these and several more international examples of nonviolence at work.

2. For a readable treatment of alternative theories of anger, see Carol Tavris's book *Anger: The Misunderstood Emotion* (Simon & Schuster / Touchstone).

3. Some will point out that the Golden Rule is only conditionally nonviolent, because it assumes that a person wants to be treated well. In the case of a person who wishes harm or destruction upon himself or herself, its usefulness as a nonviolent guideline dissolves. For example, in "suicide by police", a person violently attacks police officers because he wants the officers to kill him. However, in this section we ask readers to assume the standard interpretation of the Golden Rule. We should also note that multicultural educators, including our colleague Dr. Pamela Zappardino, prefer a revised, less ego-centric Golden Rule, which might be phrased "*Treat others as they prefer to be treated.*"

4. For an excellent treatment of violence from this perspective, see Aaron T. Beck's *Prisoners of Hate: The Cognitive Basis of Anger, Hostility, and Violence* (Harper Collins).

5. James Gilligan, M.D., an experienced prison psychiatrist and author of *Violence: Reflections on a National Epidemic* (Vintage), proposes that all violence is rooted in shame, or disrespect. Gilligan further proposes that love, guilt, fear, and knowledge of alternatives, can serve as brakes on the violence that is triggered by shame. By implication, the occurrence of violence suggests that these brakes did not work.

6. The extent to which governments seem to discount the significance of collateral damage when they go to war, appalls and often radicalizes peace advocates. An important challenge for students of nonviolence is to become more effective in pressing this issue.

Part I

Origins: Agape and Ahimsa, The Third Way

"…(In 1999) some thirty Nobel Peace Prize winners petitioned the United Nations to have the year 2000 be the beginning of a decade for education in nonviolence."

G. Simon Harak,
Nonviolence for the Third Millenium, pg. ix.

"The Ahimsa Year in 2001 celebrates the Lord Mahavira's 2600th birthday."

The Times of India, April 16, 2000.

It is ironic that in spite of wars and rumors of war in Afghanistan and Iraq, the Middle East, Sudan, Nigeria, the Congo, Northern Ireland, the former Soviet Republics, and East Timor, and notwithstanding the increased expression of rage in our society on the road, in airplanes, at sports events, and in our homes and businesses, interest in nonviolence is also increasing. In this book we have endeavored to underscore this latter trend, document its religious, spiritual, moral, and psychological underpinnings, and provide illustrations of how Agape and Ahimsa have been applied in practical situations, both personally and socially.

Martin Luther King, Jr. and Mahatma Gandhi, by way of their religious traditions, knew that there was, as Walter Wink said, "a third way" to resist evil – a way beyond violence or cowardice, flight or fight, surrender or aggression, submission or attack. King saw clearly this "third way" during his 1959 trip to India, and upon his return reflected, "The way of acquiescence leads to moral and spiritual suicide. The way of violence leads to bitterness in the survivors and brutality in the destroyers. But the way of nonviolence leads to redemption and the creation of the beloved community."[1] It was never a matter of one or the other of these options, much less whether we would resist or not. It was clearly how one would resist or in what way one would love.

King and Gandhi would not be held hostage to conventional dichotomies and easy either/or's. Rather, they transcended them and invited us to consider love and non-injury – Agape and Ahimsa – as effective forces for personal and national change, for individual peace and social justice.

Part I contains three chapters, on Agape, on Ahimsa, and on the two together as the major roots of nonviolence, the "third way". Nonviolence is not an end in itself, but a way, a path. As Nobel Peace laureate Adolfe Perez Esquival said, "Nonviolence is a lifestyle. The final objective is humanity. It is life."[2]

CHAPTER 2

Agape

Ira G. Zepp, Jr.

"Jesus is the most gracious of (persons), more gracious indeed than just a person can be. He conveys that his father in fact has no wrath. The surprise that Jesus reveals to (us) is that God is not two things at once, but that he has a single, unyielding attitude towards (us), that he loves (us) no matter what (we) do ... Jesus, through his death for those who kill him, reveals that his Father indeed cannot be pleased or offended because the Father loves (us) not for (ourselves) – were it that way there would be no love – but loves (us) because <u>He</u> is good. It is not that the Father is attracted toward (us), and drawn out of himself by (us), but that the Father, with his source of love in him rather than in us, cannot behave in any other way than to love. Jesus revealed a Father who does not react to (us), who does not put before (us) his commandments, await (our) response and then deal with (us) according to our response. He initiates love toward (us), He is the source and in no way the responder. The God whom Jesus worships as His Father, and invites us to worship similarly, is a God who is neither capricious nor arbitrary, with his power, nor scrutinizing of our behavior, in order to decide how to behave toward us." [3]

James Burtchaell,
in "The Purpose of the Church",
<u>Commonweal</u>, Sept 4, 1970, pg. 438.

THE CHRISTIAN MEANING OF AGAPE

Tucked away in the pre-Christian Greek language was a word for love rarely used before the New Testament. Early Christian writers, in their Gospels and Letters (primarily Paul and John), resurrected this heretofore obscure word, *agape*, almost untranslatable into English, to describe the outrageous, extravagant, and unconditional love revealed by God's turning toward the world in the life and death of Jesus.

To frame our discussion, I want to list several key passages in the New Testament that specifically refer to love. Every one of the following verses exemplifies a form of *agape*. And in every case, the English word "love" is a translation of *agape*. This clearly shows how indispensable *agape* was for the early Christian community – for its identity and its activity, its sense of community and its ethical behavior. The priority of *agape* is not only in its frequent use, but in its obvious centrality for the Christian understanding of God. Even more compelling is Paul's observation in Romans 13 that *agape* is the fulfillment of all religious law.

> "I give you a new commandment, that you love one another. Just as I have loved you, you also should love one another. By this everyone will know that you are my disciples, if you love one another."
>
> *John 13:34.*

> "Beloved, let us love one another, because love is from God; everyone who loves is born of God and knows God. Whoever does not love does not know God, for God is love."
>
> *I John 4:8.*

"Above all, put on love which binds things together in perfect harmony."

Colossians 3:14.

"You have heard that it was said 'You shall love your neighbor and hate your enemy. But I say to you, love your enemies and pray for those who persecute you."

Matthew 5:43-44.

"Teacher, which is the greatest commandment in the law? And Jesus said to him, 'You shall love the Lord your God with all your heart, with all your soul and with all your mind. This is the greatest and first commandment. And the second is like it. You shall love your neighbor as yourself. On these two commandments hang all the laws and prophets."

Matthew 22:36-40.
See also Mark 12:29-31 and Luke 10:27.

"The commandments ... (are) summed up in the words 'Love your neighbor as yourself.' Love does no wrong to a neighbor; therefore love is the fulfilling of the law."

Romans 13:9-10.

Finally, consider a passage from I Corinthians 13: 1-8a. This panegyric to love is unmatched in world literature. Note how love never fails; there is nothing love cannot face; love lasts forever and is the greatest of human and divine attributes:

Though I speak with the tongues of men and of angels, and have not love, I am become as sounding brass, or a tinkling cymbal.

And though I have the gift of prophecy, and understand all mysteries, and all knowledge, and though I have all faith, so that I could remove mountains, and have not love, I am nothing.

And though I bestow all my goods to feed the poor, and though I give my body to be burned, and have not love, I gain nothing.

Love is patient and kind; love is not jealous or boastful; it is not arrogant or rude. Love does not insist on its own way; it is not irritable or resentful; it does not rejoice at wrong, but rejoices in the right. Love bears all things, believes all things, hopes all things, endures all things. Love never ends...

(All the above quotations are from the 1952 Revised Standard Version of Bible.)

AGAPE AS A COMMANDMENT

The new commandment found in John 13, "that you love one another," has been called the 11th commandment. Here, and more specifically in I John 4:8, is the direct, inevitable, and necessary Biblical relationship between ontology and ethics, between the nature of God and the nature of Christian life. As God is, so people are to be. As God does, so people are to do. It is not so much that "being" precedes "doing", as we often find in philosophy, but that they are a fortunate and well-entrenched Biblical praxis – a unity of reflection and action found through the life and teachings of Jesus.

The so-called "great commandment" (to love God and neighbor), found in all three of the synoptic gospels of Matthew, Mark, and Luke, reinforces this Christian praxis. To love God with every fiber of our being is the first commandment but the second commandment is "like the first." We are to love our neighbor as ourselves. It is as if these commandments were an unstamped metallic disc, to use a Gandhian figure of speech. You don't know which side is which because the vertical and horizontal dimensions of faith are to be indelibly honed in our consciousness and expressed in our activity.

John, in the fourth chapter of his first letter, presses the issue. No one has seen God, he says. But if we love one another (not even if we love God!), God abides in us and we in God. In a real way, then, our love for one another brings God out of the abstract. That love is an icon of God, a sign and sacrament of God's presence among us. So God is made concrete and visible by our approximation of *agape*.

It is noteworthy that in much of the New Testament, love is more often used as a verb (implying dynamism) than as a noun (implying a static state). *Agape* is something we do in thankful response to God for God's love to us. This is why Soren Kierkegaard said "The Christian life is endless striving born of gratitude." Or why Isaac Watts penned "Love so amazing, so divine, demands my soul, my life, my all."

THE DIRECTIONALITY OF *AGAPE*

Agape restores a person's broken, alienated, estranged relationship with God, creating a matrix of wholeness and affecting various levels of atonement – oneness with God, self, and neighbor. This reconciling impulse is at the heart of *agape* and has inspired Christian theologians and poets to exhaust human language in describing it.

One such Christian thinker who dealt most persuasively with the theological fall-out of *agape* was Sweden's Anders Nygren in his epoch-making book, *Agape and Eros*. It is a controversial and foundational, if not revolutionary, study of what he understands the defining motif of Christianity to be.

Nygren perceives four main features of *agape*: its indifference to value while creating value; its bestowal of worth upon us rather than exacting worth from us; its spontaneity and unmotivated impulse; and its self-initiating character. *Agape* is without qualification, i.e., it is unmotivated, unconditional, undeserved, unending, unfailing. This makes *agape* radically unique and un-usual.[4]

From Nygren's perspective, *agape* is made much clearer in the distinction he makes between it and erotic love. He suggests this comparative taxonomy:[5]

Eros is acquisitive desire and longing; Agape is sacrificial giving.

Eros is an upward movement; Agape comes down.

Eros is man's way to God; Agape is God's way to man.

Eros is man's effort: it assumes that man's salvation is his work; Agape is God's grace: salvation is the work of Divine love.

Eros is egocentric love, a form of self-assertion of the highest, noblest, sublimest kind; Agape is unselfish love, it "seeks not its own," it gives itself away.

Eros seeks to gain its life, a life divine, immortalized; Agape lives the life of God, and therefore dares to "lose it."

Eros is the will to get and possess which depends on want and need; Agape is freedom in giving, which depends on wealth and plenty.

Eros is primarily *man's* love; God is the *object* of Eros. Even when it is attributed to God, Eros is patterned on human love; Agape is primarily *God's* love: God is Agape; even when it is attributed to man, Agape is patterned on Divine love.

Eros is determined by the quality, the beauty and worth, of its object; it is not spontaneous, but "evoked", "motivated"; Agape is sovereign in relation to its object, and is directed to both "the evil and the good." It is spontaneous, "overflowing," "unmotivated."

Eros *recognizes value* in its object – and loves it; Agape loves – and *creates value* in its object.

A further buttressing of Nygren's argument is made by his Swedish colleague, Gustav Aulen, who proposed in a marvelous summary of Christian atonement theories (*Christus Victor*) that the primary and preferable Christian view of atonement is the "classical" or "dramatic" theory. This theory is an explication of a verse in Paul's Corinthian correspondence in which he describes God's purpose in the suffering of Jesus on the cross. "God was in Christ reconciling the world unto himself, not counting our sins against us, but giving the message of reconciliation to us." (II Corinthians 5:19). In Christ, God, the offended and violated one, the hurt party, the one snubbed by us, takes the initiative and comes to us with an accepting and loving embrace, and in so doing absorbs and destroys all our guilt, self-pity, pride, separation, and self-elevation while not destroying the *agape* God has for us. That is the miracle and mystery of *agape*.

The cross was God's nonviolent action against all the forces of evil and injustice – sin, death, and the devil – or any opposition to God's will and purpose. Walter Wink likes to call them "principalities and powers."

God's initiating movement toward humanity radically,

cosmically, and forever alters the relation of people to God. Reconciliation has happened! Jesus died for God, on behalf of God. There was no need to satisfy God's anger or wrath because God's *agape* was self-sufficient. This is in contrast to the so-called "objective" view of the atonement promoted by Anselm a millennium ago in a little book called *Why the God-Man?* Here, Jesus died for us and sacrificed himself on our behalf, to assuage the anger, wrath, and judgment of an offended God. This has been called the substitutionary theory – Jesus taking our place, offering himself before the Holy One (the Object) as the spotless lamb of God. It is a very popular theory and has held a hegemonic dominance over Christianity for a thousand years. It is rooted in the Roman juridical system in the form of *quid pro quo* – the offering of this sacrifice or expiation in return for this benefit, e.g. forgiveness of sin. In actuality, this perverts the love of God revealed in the cross, which is fundamentally *agapaic*, i.e. self-giving and refusing to count the cost.[6]

AGAPE, AFFECTION (AND DISAFFECTION), AND WILL

The practice of *agape* is not dependent on our capacity for affection, sentiment, or emotional depth, nor on the romantic tugs and pulls of our personal lives. This is primarily why it can be commanded: You *shall* love the Lord your God … and your neighbors as yourself. This is the first and great commandment. *Agape* is not an affection; it is a matter of our will. The application of *agape* in human relationships is always "in spite of," not "because of." We will love our neighbor because God has willed it.

The covenant made by a husband and wife in marriage is a helpful human analogy. The clergy does not ask them if they are in love, if they like each other, how they feel about each other, or if they are romantically involved. Marriage is not based on a state of affection, but on a solid vow and covenant. The clergy asks "Will you love each other … in sickness and in health, in prosperity and adversity, for better or for worse?" That is to say, "When you can't stand each other, when you are on each other's nerves, when you don't like each other, will you love each other?" The response by the bride and groom is "We will."

Martin Luther King counted on this understanding of *agape* to make sense of his use of nonviolence. We are not, he said, talking about love as "emotional bosh" or "merely a sentimental outpouring" but something deeper, and that depth is to be found in *agape*.

"*Agape* is more than romantic love, *agape* is more than friendship. *Agape* is understanding, creative, redemptive good will to all men. It is an overflowing love which seeks nothing in return … So that when one rises to love on this level, he loves men not because he likes them, not because their ways appeal to him, but he loves every man because God loves him … I'm very glad (Jesus) didn't say like your enemies, because it is pretty difficult to like some people … but Jesus says love them, and love is greater than like."[7]

Nonviolence is not dependent on sentimental emotional attachment to your opponent. That would be a burden too heavy for even Jesus to bear (cf. his action against the money changers in the Temple), much less Albert Luthuli, Martin Niemoeller, Danilo Dolci, Cesar Chavez, and Dom Helder Camara in their valiant nonviolent lives of protest against injustice.

That *agape* can be commanded and willed allowed Martin Luther King to love white Americans. That love did not spring from his feeling for them, but from his spiritual direction and the will of God. And, to the extent that reconciliation exists today between the races, it is due in no small measure to King's fulfillment of this commandment of Jesus. As James Baldwin was reputed to have said to his nephew, "old buddy, if we don't love the white man, he has no hope, no atonement."

FORGIVENESS

Agape has also to do with forgiving enemies. Walter Wink, noted New Testament scholar, has said that the ultimate religious question today should no longer be (Luther's) "How can I find a gracious God?" but "How can I find God in my enemy?"[8] Loving and forgiving enemies are at the center of *agape* as well as in the heart of God. Every Christian who adheres to nonviolence must face head-on this teaching of Jesus and, if you will pardon the expression, make her or his peace with these verses. Here is the passage: "You have heard that it was said, 'An eye for an eye and a tooth for a tooth.' But I say to you, do not resist one who is evil. But if any one strikes you on the right cheek, turn to them the other, and if any one would sue you and take your coat, let them have your cloak as well; if any one forces you to go a mile, go with them two miles."[9]

Wink claims that this teaching of Jesus implies three possible responses: submission, violent opposition, or a third way which might be called nonviolent direct action. And for Wink the heart of Jesus' 'third way' is contained in the thesis statement in Matthew 5:39, "Resist not evil" (King James Version) and "Do not resist one who is evil" (Revised Standard Version).

"Resist not evil" has been the usual translation of the term *anthistemi*, But, says Wink, Jesus would have hardly advised his audience not to resist evil. "That would have been absurd. His entire ministry is utterly at odds with such a preposterous idea."[10] Perhaps the hermeneutical stance of members of the translation team, appointed by James I, was a reflection of the throne's desire to keep the king's subjects compliant and passive. In any case, Jesus' entire life was a refutation of passivity. He embodied the practice of active, initiating love. As we said earlier, it was never a case of either resistance or surrender, but in what way one would resist evil or in what way *agape* would be applied. Jesus was not about to be a co-conspirator in our victimization or our being a doormat.

So Wink suggests the following, more accurate translation of *anthistemi*: "Do not strike back at evil (or one who has done you evil) in kind. Do not give blow for blow. Do not retaliate against violence with violence. Do not resist an evil by letting the evil itself dictate the terms of your response."[11]

Martin Luther King profoundly understood this rendering of the text. In a sermon titled "Loving Your Enemies," surely one of the great statements of twentieth century Christian literature, King reminded us that there will be no permanent solution to the race problem until oppressed men develop the capacity to love their enemies. He goes on to say "Forgiveness does not mean ignoring what has been done or putting a false label on an evil act. It means, rather, that the evil act no longer remains as a barrier to the relationship. Forgiveness is a catalyst creating the atmosphere necessary for a fresh start and a new beginning ... Forgiveness means reconciliation, a coming together again."[12]

L. Gregory Jones supports this argument. "Christian forgiveness," he says, "is not simply a word of acquittal; nor is it something that merely refers backward. Rather Christian forgiveness – and, more specifically, forgiven-ness – is a way of life, a fidelity to a relationship of friendship, that must be learned and relearned in our journey toward holiness in God's eschatological Kingdom."[13]

One of the most poignant observations of the nature of agapaic forgiveness is from Miroslav Volf's recent reflections on the inter-ethnic cycles of violence in the former Yugoslavia, especially in his native Croatia, and elsewhere in the world.

"Forgiveness is the boundary between exclusion and embrace. It heals the wounds that the power-acts of exclusion have inflicted and breaks down the dividing wall of hostility. Yet it leaves a distance between people, an empty space of neutrality, that allows them either to go their separate ways in what is sometimes called 'peace' or to fall into each other's arms and restore broken communion ... At the heart of the cross is Christ's stance of not letting the other remain an enemy and creating space in himself for the offender to come in."[14]

Agape has the cathartic effect of exorcizing the demons in our relationships – the enmity, the injustice, the bitterness, the grudges, the hatred, the violence. Martin Luther King knew this all too well. But for him, forgiving the white racist was not easy, not a trivial pursuit, nor a case of sloppy *agape*. It was a costly and difficult love. And as an oppressed person, he had an epistemological advantage over the racist. King knew something his opponents did not, namely, that the white racist was just as powerless and imprisoned as the black victim of segregation, if not more so, through his historic prejudice, social programming, and self-aggrandizing egoism and could only be freed from this bondage by the victim's forgiveness.

Agape and Justice

The necessary and dialectical relation between *agape* and justice cannot be overlooked. A frequently mentioned limitation of *agape* is that it is applicable only in one-to-one relationships where self-sacrifice and indiscriminate benevolence are possible and appropriate. But, as the argument goes, when *agape* is applied in one-to-many relations, it is severely qualified. Some Protestant traditions have even made this distinction a dualism by calling justice "Law" and the Gospel "Love." Others have said that love can be practiced with the neighbor and justice only with a neighborhood. In this latter case one has then to deal with competing neighbor claims and, of necessity, is called upon to be prudential, calculating, pragmatic, and compromising.

The most helpful dialectician of love and justice was Reinhold Niebuhr (who also was one of the most influential theologians for Martin Luther King). That is to say, love and justice for Niebuhr can be distinguished but they are not to be separated, nor to be seen as different in kind. As Niebuhr said, "love is both the fulfillment and the negation of all the achievements of justice in history – fulfillment in that it serves to expand the agapaic potential of justice and negation in that it always transcends justice, to bring under judgment every realization of justice."[15]

In complex human relations of society, Niebuhr understood that the ethical goal is not love, but the achievement of justice. For love is expressed in social relationships in terms of justice. This in no way is to devalue love. Indeed, love demands justice, which is the highest approximation of love that finite human beings can realize in their social existence.

All this was not lost on King. He knew as a member of a disadvantaged group that, in his words, "the Negro needs justice, not merely love." In fact, King said, we must demand justice for Negroes. "Love that does not satisfy justice is no love at all. It is merely sentimental affection, little more than what one would have for a pet. Love at its best is justice concretized."[16] For instance, if white persons in power truly loved minorities or the dispossessed, the former would be about relinquishing the privilege of their majority status and the possessions their power had helped them obtain, and work for social justice. King knew this could be accomplished most effectively by legislation informed by love. He even got more specific, and his theology is as "realistic" as Niebuhr's. To critics who sought to diminish the effects of law he said, "Morality cannot be legislated, but behavior can be regulated."

And further, "It may be true that law can't make a man love me, but it can keep him from lynching me."

Nor was King held hostage to the setting of love over against power. "What is needed is a realization that power without love is reckless and abusive and that love without power is sentimental and anemic. Power at its best is love implementing the demands of justice. Justice at its best is love correcting everything which stands against love."[17] Since, in public policy and legislation, love is tested by justice, the higher the ideal of love, the more justice we will produce. That is the practical need for *agape* and its accompanying nonviolence, the highest human ideal and divine revelation we know. That is why Reinhold Niebuhr called *agape* a "relevant ideal." It has the magnetic power to attract us to its fulfillment and at the same time to judge our every approximation of it.

Approximations of *Agape*

Agape, by its very nature, will not be perfectly expressed in human relationships. The ideal will always be approximated and, to some degree, refracted; it would be unrealistic to expect otherwise. But it is worth paying attention to examples around us which do come relatively close to *agape*'s high standard and which provide models for our own striving. An agapaic God surely understands our inability to reach perfection.

The following illustrations are not deliberate efforts to exemplify the theology we have been discussing. As is so often the case, *agape* as well as much of God's activity, is quiet, cloaked in anonymity, and (unlike violence) the opposite of "front-page news."

The Umpire and the Second Baseman

In late September 1996, the Baltimore Orioles were playing the Toronto Blue Jays in the Skydome in Toronto. A *cause celebre* occurred during that game which will forever be recorded in the annals of baseball. After being called out on strikes by umpire John Hirshbeck, Roberto Alomar, the Orioles' second baseman, was so incensed that he spat in the umpire's face and later cast aspersions on the umpire's ability at home plate by charging that Hirshbeck's young son's death was a source of unbearable stress for him. Indeed, Hirshbeck's two sons, John Drew, the one who died, and Michael, still living, had both been afflicted from an early age with a serious degenerative disorder called adrenoleukodystrophy (ALD). Hirshbeck allegedly cussed at Alomar and threatened to kill him. For two years, the enraged official and player avoided each other's presence as much as humanly possible.

Alomar was eventually traded to the Cleveland Indians in the winter of 1999 and would continue to be near Hirshbeck, who not only lived near Cleveland but also remained an American League umpire.

After prodding from Jack Efta, a mutual friend, and Sandy Alomar, the Cleveland catcher and Roberto's brother, the two men seemed ready for some form of reconciliation. But it was Hirshbeck who took the initiative in another September game in Cleveland in 1999 to talk with Roberto. After a brief conversation, they decided to let the ugly incident rest. "If that's the worst thing Robbie ever does in his life, he'll lead a real good life. People make mistakes. You forgive, you forget, and move on," said Hirshbeck.

Alomar's response was to donate more than fifty thousand dollars to a foundation which is helping to find a cure for ALD. "We're not here to hold grudges, we're here to help people. Hopefully, someday a miracle will happen and we can find a cure for John's son. That would be the happiest day of my life, because I had helped somebody."[18]

Loving Your Enemies

Consider this response of Martin Luther King to the Ku Klux Klan and other violent persons:

"My friends, we have followed the so-called practical way for too long a time now, and it has led inexorably to deeper confusion and chaos. Time is cluttered with the wreckage of communities which surrendered to hatred and violence. For the salvation of our nation and the salvation of mankind, we must follow another way. This does not mean that we abandon our righteous efforts. With every ounce of our energy we must continue to rid this nation of the incubus of segregation. But we shall not in the process relinquish our privilege and our obligation to love. While abhorring segregation, we shall love the segregationist. This is the only way to create the beloved community. To our most bitter opponents we say, 'We shall match your capacity to inflict suffering by our capacity to endure suffering. We shall meet your physical force with soul force. Do to us what you will, and we shall continue to love you. We cannot in all good conscience obey your unjust laws, because non-cooperation with evil is as much a moral obligation as is cooperation with good. Throw us in jail, and we shall still love you. Send your hooded perpetrators of violence into our community at the midnight hour and beat us and leave us half dead, and we shall still love you. But be ye assured that we will wear you down by our capacity to suffer. One day we shall win freedom, but not only for ourselves. We shall so appeal to your heart and conscience that we shall win you in the process, and our victory will be a double victory.'"

The Forgotten Baptism

Several years ago one of us (Ira) scheduled a baptism of a child whose parents were former students and whose wedding I had performed. The baptism was set for the Sunday afternoon following Thanksgiving in our College Chapel. That very afternoon I took my son back, after his Thanksgiving break, to Washington College on Maryland's eastern shore, almost two hours from our home and the College in Westminster, MD. I had missed a most important day in the lives of two young people and the fifty or more persons there in the Chapel for the baptism.

When it was determined that I was not going to be there, the somewhat anxious couple called our home and our oldest son took the message. Well, he happened to know through a college friend about another nearby minister and phoned him to see if he could come and fill in for me. He did so in graceful fashion. When I returned home and received the news, I was in shock. The agapaic nature of this event is that the disappointed and forgotten Cindy and Carter not only forgave me, but asked that I have the baptism of their next two children. It was one of the most profound experiences of *agape* I ever had. It was truly undeserved, unconditional, and unforgettable. I had no words to express my gratitude.

Nonviolent Love Under German Occupation[20]

An old Huguenot community in France, Le Chambon-sur-Lignon, was spared destruction in World War II under interesting circumstances. The townspeople had committed themselves to Christian nonviolence, and, though under German occupation, actively assisted many Jews in escaping to Switzerland. The town leaders and the German military played cat-and-mouse for an extended period of time; an informer apparently kept the town prepared for "surprise" inspections.

But on one occasion, the town doctor went to visit the local military commandant to plead for the release of a young townsman who had been arrested. In the course of his interview, the doctor explained the town's nonviolent approach to the war, and his people's belief that the Germans were doing hateful things, but were not inherently evil people. Unrelated to this meeting, a crime occurred that day near the military headquarters, and strict security was imposed. The doctor's driver was found to have a forbidden weapon in his car, which led to the doctor's arrest and eventual execution.

The commandant, however, had been impressed and moved by what the doctor had told him. When captured and interrogated at the end of the war, he revealed that he had refused to allow Le Chambon-sur-Lignon to be razed by the Gestapo. The doctor's account of the town's philosophy, and other behavior of the townspeople toward his soldiers, had convinced him that there was something good about Le Chambon: "I do not understand these people. But I have talked with them and I know that they do not hate us. They are not killers. They are not in the movement of violence."

Moral Jui-Jitsu

Richard Gregg, who was greatly influenced by Gandhi, has outlined some of the essential psychological and moral mechanisms at work in nonviolent resistance. A chapter of his book, *The Power of Nonviolence*, is entitled "Moral Jui-Jitsu."[21] In physical jui-jitsu, the aim is to destroy the sense of balance in the opponent while retaining one's own balance. In moral jui-jitsu the opponent loses his moral balance and therefore becomes a potential convert to the position of the nonviolent resister. For our purposes here, we see how the technique of "moral jui-jitsu" as employed by Gandhi and by King threw off balance the United Kingdom and the United States. How this occurs is summarized by Gregg.

First, the victim is sincerely willing to suffer and not to inflict suffering. If a blow is returned for a blow, the initial attacker is, paradoxically, reassured, and has received a kind of moral validation. The victim's scale of values, then becomes an echo of the attacker's. But if the victim decides to suffer and not to react violently, "the attacker loses the moral support which the usual violent resistance of most victims would render him. He plunges forward, as it were, into a new world of values." Second, the attacker is thrown off balance, surprised, "loses his pose, and may become confused in his thinking and, in short, is rendered incapable of action. In this new world of values, his instincts no longer tell him instantly what to do."[22]

Something very similar to this happened in the 1963 Birmingham campaign under the leadership of Martin Luther King. A group of African-Americans wanted to have a prayer meeting near the city jail and began to assemble there. The Superintendent of Public Safety, Bull Connor, told his officers to turn water hoses on the marchers. As King related, "What happened in the next thirty seconds was one of the most fantastic events in the Birmingham story. Bull Connor's men, their deadly hoses poised for action, stood facing the marchers. The marchers, many of them on their knees, stared back, unafraid and unmoving. Slowly, the Negroes stood up and began to advance. Connor's men, as though hypnotized, fell back, their hoses sagging uselessly in their hands while several hundred Negroes marched past them without further interference, and held their prayer meeting as planned."[23]

A Different Kind of Justice

How could South Africa heal the horror, brutality, and agony of apartheid? In the mid-1990's, a relatively unique experiment in public policy took place by the creation of the Truth and Reconciliation Commission (TRC) headed by Bishop Desmond Tutu. It "went beyond the limitations of secular law, exploring new potentials for forgiveness and national reconciliation – themes that are increasingly relevant internationally."[24]

Here are some insights (which to us are riveting) about the TRC experiment, from Peter Storey's account in *The Christian Century*:

> "Precedents for such an investigation – in post-war Germany or in Central and Latin America – offered more warnings than guidance. They showed that when cruelty becomes national policy, law alone is not enough. Nuremberg dispensed harsh retribution to the top echelon of Nazi butchers, but ignored their victims and allowed ordinary Germans to live in a state of denial…"

> "Rather than denying justice, the TRC process may be exploring justice in a larger, more magnanimous form – what Charles Villa-Vicencio calls restorative justice as opposed to retributive justice. Perhaps this unique exercise points beyond conventional retribution into a realm where justice and mercy coalesce and both victim and perpetrator must know pain if healing is to happen. It is an area more consistent with Calvary than the courtroom. It is the place where the guilty discover the pain of forgiveness because the innocent are willing to bear the greater pain of forgiving."

SUMMING UP

It is difficult to capture the full meaning of *agape* briefly. However, here is a distillation derived from the selection of observations we have made to this point. *Agape* is a profound form of love that is extended toward others simply because they are fellow human beings. Not surprisingly, this love is tested most severely by oppression, injustice, and cruelty perpetrated by others. The expression of agape occurs at the initiation of the offended party. When the one violated, when the hurt party, takes the first step in the reconciling process, nonviolent direct action is being employed. This is the inherent logic of *agape*; it leads inevitably and without hesitation to nonviolence and to a more profound atonement, reconciliation, and justice, than if a lesser ideal of love were to have been applied.

Notes

1. Martin Luther King, Jr., "My Trip to India" pg. 5. Boston Collection. Arthur G. Gish also called for a "third alternative" between acquiescence to injustice and violent revolution in his The New Left and Christian Radicalism, Grand Rapids, Eerdmans, 1970, pg. 139.

2. Quoted in Sojourners, Dec. 1986 pg. 32.

3. Burtchaell, James, "The Purpose of the Church," Commonweal, Sept. 4, 1970, pg. 438.

4. For an extended discussion, see Nygren, Anders, Agape and Eros, New York, Harper Torch Books, 1953, pp. 75-81.

5. Agape and Eros, pg. 210. There has been a good deal of criticism of this comparison as simplistic and reductionist. Philia, another Greek word for love, having to do with reciprocity in human relations, mutuality in friendship, and neighborly companionship, is often used as a mediating link between eros and agape. Martin King often made use of this trifurcation of love in his sermons and essays to defend the notion that agape is a viable force for nonviolence. Nevertheless, with this comparison, Nygren helps us see what Christianity claims to be the unique essence of God. While being holy and wrathful, God is not finally that; God is finally love. For a more systematic critique of Nygren, see Outak, Gene, Agape: An Ethical Analysis, New Haven and London, Yale University Press, 1973, and for a brilliant review of Outak's book, see Religious Studies Review, Vol. 1, Sept 1975, pp. 25-29.

6. See Aulen, Gustav, Christus Victor, London, SPCK, 1953, pp. 162-167. The purpose of this distinction between the "classical theory" and the "substitutionary theory" is that, generally speaking, those who subscribe to the latter theory do not support nonviolence as a way of life.

7. "Love, Law, and Civil Disobedience" in <u>A Testament of Hope:</u> <u>The Essential Writings of Martin Luther King, Jr.</u>, edited by James Washington, Harper and Row, San Francisco, 1986, pp. 46-47.

8. <u>Sojourners</u>, Nov 1986, pg. 15. <u>Sojourners</u> published a series of four articles by Wink from Nov 1986 to Feb 1987 on the subject of nonviolent resistance to evil.

9. <u>Matthew</u> 5:38-41. I am very much indebted to Wink for his exegetical insights into these verses. See also <u>Matthew</u> 5:44-45: "You have heard that it was said, 'You shall love your neighbor and hate your enemy,' But I say to you, love your enemies and pray for those who persecute you." It is obvious that this agapaic love for enemies is the foundation for forgiving them, i.e. turning the other cheek, going the second mile. It is also apparent that Wink does not feel that these "hard teachings" of Jesus are the "interim ethic" of Albert Schweitzer or the "counsel of perfection" of Roman Catholic monasticism or the "impossible possibility" of Reinhold Niebuhr. Wink, along with Martin King and Gandhi, takes these words of Jesus as practical and possible guidelines for Christian living.

10. <u>Sojourners</u>, Dec 1986, pg. 29

11. <u>Sojourners</u>, Dec 1986, pg. 29 and <u>Sojourners</u>, Nov 1986, pg. 15. See also the conclusion of the Apostle Paul's summary of the Sermon on the Mount (especially <u>Matthew</u> 5), in <u>Romans</u> 12:21. "Do not be overcome by evil, but overcome evil with good."

12. Martin Luther King, Jr., <u>Strength to Love</u>, Philadelphia, Fortress Press, 1981, pg. 50-51.

13. Jones, L. Gregory, <u>Embodying Forgiveness: A Theological Analysis</u>, Grand Rapids, Eerdmans Publishing Co., 1995, pg. 66. See also pp. 195-196.

14. Volf, Miroslav, <u>Exclusion and Embrace: A Theological Exploration of Identity, Otherness, and Reconciliation</u>. Nashville, Abingdon Press, 1996, pp.275-306.

15. Zepp, Ira G. Jr., <u>The Social Vision of Martin Luther King, Jr.</u>,

Brooklyn, Carlson Publishing , 1989, pp. 148-150.

16. King, Martin Luther Jr., <u>Where Do We Go From Here: Chaos or Community?</u> New York, Harper and Row Publishers, 1967, pp. 89-90.

17. <u>Ibid</u>., pg. 37.

18. See <u>The Baltimore Sun</u>, "Score One for Friendship", by Ken Rosenthal, 10/17/99, pg. 1A and 4A.

19. King, Martin Luther Jr., <u>Strength to Love</u>, Philadelphia, Fortress Press, 1981, pg. 56.

20. The following is adapted from Ferguson, John, <u>The Politics of Love: The New Testament and Nonviolent Revolution</u>, NY, Fellowship Publications, 1979, pp. 105-106.

21. Gregg, Richard, <u>The Power of Nonviolence</u>, Second Revised Edition, NY, Schocken Books, 1966. See especially, pp. 43-46.

22. For a full exposition of this method, see Zepp, <u>The Social Vision of Martin Luther King, Jr.</u>, pp. 102-103.

23. King, Martin Luther, Jr., <u>Why We Can't Wait</u>, NY, Harper and Row, 1963, pp. 107-108.

24. Peter Storey in "A Different Kind of Justice: Truth and Reconciliation in South Africa"; from <u>The Christian Century</u>, Sept 10-17, 1997, pg. 788. I have excerpted two paragraphs from Storey's article to give a sense of the TRC's impact on South Africa and the world. An appreciative, yet critical, perspective on the TRC is found in a review by Sara Ruden of Desmond Tutu's book, <u>No Future Without Forgiveness</u>, in <u>The Christian Century</u>, July 5-12, 2000, pp. 722-725.

CHAPTER 3

Ahimsa

Ira G. Zepp, Jr.

I hold that nonviolence is not merely a personal virtue. It is also a social virtue to be cultivated like the other virtues. Surely, society is largely regulated by the expression of non-violence in its mutual dealings. What I ask for is an extension of it on a larger, national and international scale. The love that Jesus taught and practiced was not a mere personal virtue, but it was essentially a social and collective virtue. Buddha taught and practiced the same thing six hundred years before Jesus.

Gandhi, Harijan, March 4, 1939.

Q. Does anyone know true non-violence?

A. Nobody knows it, for nobody can practice perfect non-violence… Perfect non-violence is impossible so long as we exist physically, for we would want some space at least to occupy. Perfect non-violence, while you inhabit the body, is only a theory like Euclid's point or straight line, but we have to endeavor every moment of our lives.

Gandhi, Harijan, July 21, 1940.

HISTORICAL BACKGROUND
The precise origin of *ahimsa* is lost in the mist of pre-historical India and only obliquely mentioned in the *Vedas*, Hinduism's oldest scriptures. The *Upanishads* are threaded with the mantra

of peace and in that scripture *ahimsa* is considered one of the priestly gifts (see especially the *Chandogya Upanishad*). In the *Yoga Sutra* of Patanjali, *ahimsa* is viewed as one of the yogic restraints.[1] In neither text, however, is ahimsa systematically delineated.

Ahimsa, as the highest Hindu ethical virtue, i.e. non-injury and refraining from violence in thought and action, was first brought to our consciousness and initially recorded in the religions of Lord Mahavira (c.599-572 BCE) and the Buddha (c.560-480 BCE) who founded, respectively, Jainism and Buddhism, both sixth/fifth century BCE Hindu reform movements. While, concurrently, the Greek mathematician and philosopher Pythagoras was developing a theory of nonviolence, it never took hold in Greek culture or religion in the same way it did in these two Indian religions.

Jainism, at its most orthodox, is a religion of world negation, *par excellence*, but a religion in which that negation acquires a strong ethical bent. This purified form of Hinduism has influenced Indian thought and life out of all proportion to its size (about 2-3 million adherents) within India's population of one billion people). It was a strong religious force in Gandhi's home state of Gujurat and his mother's Jain leanings made an indelible imprint on his life. Jainism also provided for Gandhi the benefits and strengths of authentic asceticism and the values of fasting and other spiritual vows, which fueled his desire for perfection.

The basis of Jain ethics is *ahimsa*, etymologically from Sanskrit roots: *Han* meaning to kill or to do harm, and *Him*, the desire to kill. A-himsa is the refusal to kill and refusal to do harm. At the heart of this precept is the radical commitment to refrain from harming any living being, i.e. not to kill, misuse, insult, torment, or persecute any form of created life.[2]

As one would imagine, this has profound consequences for

the daily life of a devout Jain believer. During my Fulbright travels to India, especially in the holy city of Varanasi (formerly called Benares), I saw Jain monks carrying brooms to sweep the path before their footsteps and wearing cloth masks over their nose and mouth so they would not, in either case, inadvertently tramp on, swallow or otherwise destroy insects or even smaller other microorganisms. It was for this reason, as well, that Gandhi for fear of walking accidentally on insects, often shuffled around his ashram floors. Furthermore, Jains would not hunt and refrained from farming because it was impossible to either plow or till the soil without harming the smallest of living creatures. So they are vegetarians, and in some cases eat only the part of the plant that can be gleaned above the ground. Lord Mahavira summed up the rigors of Jain discipleship in the "Five Great Vows." They were meant for monks and other ascetics but were applicable, in varying degrees, to all Jain believers. For all the latter, non-injury is the priority of the religious life and the centerpiece of the first vow. One notices immediately how *ahimsa* and all the other vows are grounded in renunciation, or what Gandhi called "selflessness."

Here is a summary of the five vows:[3]

1. *I renounce all killing of living beings, whether movable or unmovable. Nor should I myself kill living beings nor cause others to do so, nor consent to it.* This vow is first not only chronologically, but also first in terms of its significance for Jainism. Voorst reminds us that unmovable living beings are understood to be earth, water, fire, wind, grass, trees, and plants. Movable beings are both egg-bearing or those that bear live offspring and those generated from dirt and those generated in fluids. We are to understand that they all desire happiness and by hurting these beings, people

do harm to their own souls, and will, repeatedly, be born as one of them.

2. *I renounce all vices of lying speech arising from anger or greed or fear or mirth.* Gandhi was clear that nonviolence applied to thought, word, and deed – to our attitudes as well as our actions. For him, *ahimsa* was integrated into the totality of our being – our body, mind, and spirit; there was not compartmentalization here. Gandhi summed up Jain and Buddhist teaching by saying that *Ahimsa* is "hurt by every evil thought, by undue haste, by lying, by hatred, by wishing ill to any body."[4]

3. *I renounce all taking of anything not given, either in a village or in a town or in a wood.* Here is the religious sanction for begging, practiced by many Jain monks. There arose a symbiotic relation between the begging monk and the lay community; the former were expected to beg and the latter were expected to give. In each case, karmic law was being fulfilled.

4. *I renounce all sexual pleasure. I shall not give way to sensuality, nor cause others to do so, nor consent to it in others.* This is the source of Gandhi's understanding of how compatible the vow of celibacy (*Brahmacharya*) was with the vow of nonviolence. The energy necessary for sexual activity was to be sublimated and added to the much needed energy pool for nonviolent practice.

5. *I renounce all attachments, whether to little or much, small or great, living or lifeless things.* Nothing was more influential on Gandhi. He intuited the corollary Buddhist insight that the more you have, the more you are had; the more you possess, the more you are possessed. The predication

of the observing of *ahimsa* is holding nothing of your own and being property-less. "Having,", a form of bondage itself, also requires extra effort for protection and security. This eventuated in a vow of non-possession which Gandhi required every *Satyagrahi* to take.[5]

Obviously, not every Jain can practice all the above, but most try to follow the first vow of *ahimsa* as much as they can. A twelfth century Jain poet, Hemachandra, in this hymn in praise of *ahimsa*, presents *ahimsa* as the ideal of human life and shows how central non-injury is to Jain devotees.

❑   *Ahimsa* is like a loving mother of all beings.

❑   *Ahimsa* is like a stream of nectar in the desert of Samara.

❑   *Ahimsa* is a course of rain clouds to the forest fire of suffering.

❑   The best herb of healing for the beings tormented by the disease called the perpetual returns of existence, is *Ahimsa*.[6]

Buddhism, a sister religion to Jainism, has a very similar perspective on nonviolence. After a six-year quest for clarity and life's meaning, Buddha, now fully awake, declared Four Noble Truths:

1.   All life is suffering.

2.   The cause of suffering is desire (craving).

3.   The aim of life is to overcome (renounce) desire.

4.   We renounce by following the Noble Eightfold Path.

This path is a kind of balanced, moderate form of mental

and moral purification which includes right speech, right mindfulness, right effort, right livelihood, right concentration, right vocation, right intent, and right view. "Right effort" or "right conduct" is of particular interest to us. There are five precepts which help the Buddhist follow this path and the primary precept is: Do not kill. This is not as radically applied to all living creatures as in Jainism, but it does extend beyond human life to animal life and means that Buddhists are also vegetarians. Personal prayer and meditation help Buddhists overcome hostility, resentment, and violence and produces in their lives a high level of benevolence, compassion, and nonviolence.[7]

Another influential Hindu scriptural resource for nonviolence is found in the *Bhagavad-Gita* (The Song of the God), which is section 6 of the Mahabharata, the longest epic poem in world literature. There is hardly a more poignant reflection on the nature of war and its consequences than in the *Gita*. The *Gita* was read by Gandhi as a young man while he was studying in London and its message had an immeasurable impact on him. The historical basis for the story in this most loved, but relatively brief text, is the rivalry between the brothers of the Pandava and the Kasurava families. The leader of the Pandavas lost his chance to rule India by lots which were cast in favor of the Kasuravas. Within a few years, civil war broke out.

The high god Krishna was the charioteer of Arjuna, a member of the Kshatriya caste. There is some irony in the fact that Krishna and Arjuna along with Rama, Mahavira and Buddha (the latter two, being founders of two of the world's most peaceful religions) were Kshatriyas (warrior caste). It should be remembered, however, that Mahavira wanted to reform Hinduism's sacrificial system, which involved the killing of many animals, and Buddha wanted to abolish its rigid caste system, which bound persons by virtue of birth to certain social classes. As a result of these reformations, the Jains eliminated the ritual sacrifice of animals in the name of *ahimsa* and Buddhists eradicated caste, which meant that Kshatriyas were liberated to practice peace, not war. So Arjuna's caste dharma (duty) was to fight. But Arjuna, upon reflecting what this fratricidal war would mean, debated vigorously with Krishna and wanted to forego his caste duty to fight. He concluded that this war was ill advised, dead wrong, and that he would not do battle.

But Krishna, also known for his debating skills, argued that (1) physical death cannot hurt the inner and essential soul, the Atman, and (2) at the end of the day, Arjuna, a warrior, must above all fulfill his duty. The upshot of the argument is that nonviolence seemed more suitable for the Brahman (priestly) caste than for the Kshatriyas. Be that as it may, Arjuna finally succumbed to Krishna's wishes and followed his caste duty, much against his better judgment. Of interest to us, however, is how Gandhi transposed Arjuna's Kshatriyan dharma or duty into a spiritual warfare and said it is our duty to resist, to fight, the spiritual power of our ego, greed, and inner violence. The battlefield is our soul, Gandhi said, not Kurikshetra.

However, there are in the first pages of the *Gita* some stunning anti-violent messages which reinforced Gandhi's philosophy of *ahimsa*. Listen to Arjuna's pleas:

> In killing my brothers, Krishna
> I cannot see anything noble.
> I do not want this, this glory, this happiness.
> I would not kill them,
> Not for the three worlds, let alone the earth, O Krishna.
> I'd rather they killed me.
> What joy is there in slaying Dhritarashtra's sons?

It is a terrible sin.
I will not kill my kinsmen, O Madhava.
How could happiness be mine if I murder my brothers?
We have heard, Krishna.
Hell awaits the families which discard dharma.
What a terrible sin it is to kill brothers,
And cast covetous eyes to their land.
Let the sons of Dhritarashtra kill me.
I will not protest.
Better be killed than kill.[8]

Gandhi was an inevitable heir of this inescapable and rich spiritual legacy: the *ahimsa* of Jainism, the compassion of the Buddha, and the non-violent reflections of Arjuna. It was in the air he breathed, in the words he heard from his mother, in the lives of the reformers he admired from the West, i.e., Jesus, Thoreau, Ruskin, and Tolstoy. Furthermore, Gandhi had this miraculous way of appropriating the very best from Hinduism and Christianity to support and fuel his commitment to personal purity and social justice.

Ahimsa as the Grand Law of Love
We fail to understand Gandhi's unfailing trust in *Ahimsa* if we do not see his perspective on it as a cosmic, divine, and human law which is proved in our attempts to defy it. This rule sustains all life on earth and literally makes the world go around. It is the adhesive tape which holds everything together.

Gandhi's evidence for this is that harmoniously working societies are based on the law of nonviolence. He noticed that "life persists in the midst of destruction, therefore there must be a higher law than that of destruction."[9] Gandhi insisted this law would work, just as dependably as the law of gravitation works, whether we accept it or not. "And just as a scientist will work wonders out of various applications of the Law of Nature, even a man who applies the Law of Love with scientific precision can work greater wonders. For the force of nonviolence is infinitely more wonderful and subtle than the force of nature, like, for instance, electricity. The more efficient a force is, the more silent it is. Love is the subtlest force in the world."[10]

Western readers should note that Gandhi's definition of *Ahimsa* as "love" is uniquely his. None of the other classic Indian texts nor their commentators appear to call *Ahimsa* "love;"; it is almost always "non-injury". So our discussion of *Ahimsa* is heavily driven by Gandhi's rendering of it as found in his writings. And it is arguably the influence of the personal and loving God of Christianity on Gandhi in combination with an impersonal and unchanging Brahman which provided his working definition of *Ahimsa*: love with inexorability. One sees Gandhi uniting these in so much of his writing.[11] He unhesitatingly and positively, compares I Corinthians 13, Paul's famous chapter on Love, to *Ahimsa*. "The true rendering of (*Ahimsa*) in English is love or charity. Does not the Bible say 'Love worketh no ill to its neighbor. Believeth all things, Hopeth all things, (It) never faileth.' "[12] Gandhi used similar language. "*Satyagraha* is gentle, it never wounds. It must not be the result of anger or malice. It is never fussy, never impatient, never vociferous. It is the direct opposite of compulsion."

The Law of Love was for Gandhi the Highest Good, the *Summum Bonum* and the most powerful force in the world. His entire life was a living, breathing experiment to see how far a human being could go to embody nonviolence. Remember that the sub-title of his autobiography is "The Story of My Experiments with Truth." His practice of nonviolence was in the public laboratory for all to observe. The test tube and the ingredients he used were visible to all and no one before or since has been so scrupulously honest in working out an ethical ideal. Gandhi tried and tested it, with successes and failures, and eventually smoothed out most of the wrinkles. India was the moral laboratory in which these scientific, empirically based experiments were conducted.

The Mahatma was seeking for just as much undeniable verification and proof for his experiments (conclusions) as Francis Bacon and Isaac Newton were in the laws of physics. What Natural Law was for western philosophers from Aristotle to the Enlightenment, the Law of *Ahimsa* was for Gandhi. What the will of God is for Jews, Christians, and Muslims, *Ahimsa* was for Gandhi.

The "grand" nature of this Law of Love is that we love those who do not love us. Gandhi is quick to state how this teaching is strikingly reminiscent of Jesus who said "If you love those who love you, what reward have you. Even sinners do that." (Matthew 5:46). Love of the hater is the most difficult of all, said Gandhi.

In the beginning of the last decade of his life, Gandhi wrote, "I have an implicit faith – faith that today burns brighter than even half a century's experience of unbroken practice of nonviolence – that mankind can only be saved through nonviolence which is the central teaching of the Bible as I understand the Bible."[13]

SATYAGRAHA: AHIMSA'S ONTOLOGICAL REALITY

Let us examine the multi-textured principle of *Satyagraha*. "*Sat*" has several overlapping meanings in Sanskrit – Spirit, Soul, Truth, God, Love – all of which could be summed up in its root meaning of "Being." "*Graha*" also has many aspects – commitment, devotion, holding, grasping, force – all of which might be summed up in its root meaning, "firmness."

So *Satyagraha* is firmness in the Truth, holding on to Truth. Gandhi liked to call it "Soul Force" when he discussed nonviolence. Martin Luther King Jr. used the same translation quite often in his essays and sermons.

For Gandhi, the opposite of Truth is violence, because the ultimate value (God, Brahman, Being itself) is a loving, nonviolent, peaceful, Truthful reality. Therefore, violence has no ontological ground on which to stand. There is no support for it in the very heart of the universe and thus in the human heart. Gandhi captured this notion in a classic passage to a friend in 1932. "In 'God is Truth,' *is* certainly does not mean 'equal to' nor does it merely mean 'is truthful'. Truth is not a mere attribute of God, but He is That. He is nothing if He is not That. Truth in Sanskrit means *Sat*. *Sat* means is. Therefore, Truth is implied in Is. God is, nothing else is. Therefore, the more Truthful we are, the nearer we are to God. We are only to the extent that we are truthful."[14] The metaphysical nature of *Satyagraha* had, for Gandhi, at the same time (1) an ethical dimension, e.g., a mode of action called nonviolent resistance, and (2) an epistemological aspect, e.g., a method of inquiry which resulted in his life-long experiments in Truth.

Bondurant has some very helpful definitions for those who wish to apply *Satyagraha*. Gandhi would certainly have agreed with these insights of hers.

❑   Force – power to exercise influence and to effect change.

❑   Violence – to do anything so as to intentionally injure a person or thing.

❑   Injury – harm done to another either psychologically or physically.

❑ Nonviolence – *Satyagraha* – to effect change without injury to an adversary.[15]

Since *Satyagraha* is something done and not said, Gandhi was obsessed to put it into practice. His burning questions were:

How to move most authentically (Truthfully) from metaphysics to ethics?

How to actualize in history the ideal of Truth?

How to make his mystical vision politically relevant?

How to ethicize the ontology of Truth?

For all these reasons, the first vow of the *Satyagrahi* (one who practices *Satyagraha*) was Truth. In essence, it was a religious profession, a precept rooted in God.[16] However Truth-full we might be, we can only approximate the Brahmanic or Godly ideal. It is humanly impossible to know the Truth absolutely and because of that we cannot afford the luxury of being violent or being able to punish. This is why "means" are so pivotal for Gandhi, about which more later.

The Apparently Negative is Actually Positive

Many commentators have focused on the "A" in *Ahimsa*, i.e. they have stressed non-injury, non-killing, non-violence, etc., and concluded that *Ahimsa* is inherently a negative action or passive reaction. Many Indian linguists and historians corroborate this. *Ahimsa* was generally construed as a negative principle, what you do *not* do, notwithstanding that *Satyagraha*, on which *Ahimsa* is based, has positive connotations. Remember it is holding on to Truth, doing the Truth, being firm in the Truth.

And Gandhi is quite clear. Refraining from hurting others is a positive action. "*Ahimsa* does not simply mean non-killing.

Himsa means causing pain to or killing any life out of anger or from a selfish purpose, or with the intention of injuring it. Refraining from so doing is *Ahimsa*."[17]

Over and over again, Gandhi said that *Ahimsa* was not only not negative, it was a spirit, a way of life, the law of one's being; it was love, a love which springs from nonviolence and therefore could never be simply negative or re-active. Personally, it meant loving those who don't love you and politically it meant setting one's whole being against, as in Gandhi's case, the rigidity of the caste system and the colonial power and imperial rule of Great Britain.

MEANS AND ENDS

The relation of means to ends is at the core of Gandhi's nonviolent methodology. It was never, as in *realpolitik*, where the end justifies the means, nor even in Malcolm X's aphorism "by any means necessary." For Gandhi, the end pre-existed in the means; or that is, the means you use will determine the actual end you achieve. One cannot emphasize enough the dynamic, inevitable link Gandhi saw between ends and means. They are irrevocably bound together. This idea appears and reappears in his writing; here are a few examples which typify this tip of an iceberg.

❑ "fair means alone can produce fair results."

❑ "means and ends are convertible terms in my philosophy of life."

❑ "They say 'means are after all only means.' I would say 'means are after all everything.' "[18]

There is no dividing wall between *Ahimsa* and *Satyagraha*, no separation between nonviolence (means) and Truth (end).

There may be a distinction, but there is no difference. As Gandhi once said, "*Ahimsa* and Truth are my two lungs. I cannot live without them."[19]

With more detailed specificity, Gandhi outlined his position. "Without *Ahimsa* it is not possible to seek and find Truth. *Ahimsa* and Truth are so intertwined that it is practically impossible to disentangle them and separate them. They are like the two sides of a coin, or rather of a smooth unstamped metallic disc. Who can say which is the obverse and which is the reverse? Nevertheless *Ahimsa* is the means, Truth is the end … If one takes care of the means, we are bound to reach the end sooner or later. When once we have grasped this point, final victory is beyond question."[20]

There is consummate good sense and compelling logic in Gandhi's contention that means and ends co-inhere. Wars do not create peace; choosing such a means for arriving at such a goal is self-incriminating from the start. The value of wars is that they may result in the cessation of physical hostility or halt violence and in our finite world that is no mean achievement; but wars do not create nonviolence. Peaceful means are the way to peaceful ends. Love is the way to love. To the extent that we have a racially integrated society in the United States, it is largely due to the means employed by Martin Luther King Jr. and the Civil Rights Movement. The extent to which Anglo-Indian relations were as amicable as they were when Britain was forced to leave the brightest jewel in its crown, was contingent on the amicable methods used by Gandhi and the Quit India Movement.

This theme of the necessary link between ends and means is rooted in Buddhism, whose peaceful teachings Gandhi treasured. In the *Dhammapada*, Buddha says "Hatred never ceases hatred. Violence never ceases by violence. This is eternal law."[21] A cursory reading of Martin Luther King will discover how heavily he was indebted to Gandhi for this insight into his own articulation of nonviolence.

AHIMSA AND BRAVERY

It dies hard that advocates of nonviolence are said to be braver than practitioners of violence, that soul force requires more courage than the force of arms. Here Gandhi wants us to do a flip-flop of language and place ordinary understanding on its head. Popular opinion often attributes cowardice, weakness, and timidity to nonviolence. Gandhi wanted to face this issue head-on and claim that taking up arms is the sign of weakness and that nonviolence and cowardice are contradictory, inconsistent, and oxymoronic. This is one of the most repeated themes in his addresses and newspaper columns. Here is a sample of the essence of this principle.

❑ "A man cannot then practice *Ahimsa* and be a coward at the same time."[22]

❑ "Nonviolence is not a cover for cowardice, but it is also the supreme virtue of the brave. Exercise of nonviolence requires far greater bravery than that of swordsmanship."[23]

❑ "My creed of nonviolence is an extremely active force. It has no room for cowardice or even weakness. There is hope for a violent man to be some day nonviolent, but there is none for a coward."[24]

One of Gandhi's most compelling observations in this regard is the following: "Wherein is courage required –- in blowing others to pieces from behind a cannon, or with a smiling face to approach a cannon to be blown to pieces? Who is the true warrior – he who keeps death always as a bosom friend or he who controls the death of others?"[25] Gandhi's distinction is uncomplicated. There is a vast moral difference between those who are willing to inflict suffering and those who are willing to suffer. A person who is afraid of death is not equipped to resist successfully. If one does not fear death, that person is invincible and threatens any adversary.

But Gandhi was never an ideologue about this. He said on one occasion: "I would rather have India resort to arms in order to defend her honor than that she would in a cowardly manner become or remain a helpless witness to her own dishonor. But I believe that nonviolence is infinitely superior to violence, forgiveness is more manly than punishment."[26]

So we see that Gandhi never accepted cowardly flight; he preferred violence to cowardice if these were the only options available. He once said that he could no more preach nonviolence to a coward than he could tempt a blind man to enjoy healthy sight. A useful frame of reference to understand more fully the logic of Gandhi's discussion of nonviolence and bravery is to see it in the context of what he called the nonviolence of the strong and the nonviolence of the weak. What gives credibility to the personal convictions and integrity to the practice of nonviolence is the direct correlation between the ability, *not the will*, of the nonviolent person to inflict injury. They are able to strike back, but *will* not to do so. That is their strength. The credibility of the nonviolence of the strong is predicated on the ability to be violent, to strike with physical force. This person has made a conscious decision to refuse revenge. This is the nonviolence of the strong. If the person was unable to strike because of personal or military weakness, that would not be *Satyagraha*; it would be the nonviolence of the weak. Gandhi's life and teaching re-enforces the notion that it takes an immense amount of courage to be nonviolent and a proportionate amount of cowardice to be violent.

AHIMSA AND RENUNCIATION

Ahimsa has its source in the *sine qua non* of the Jain religion – willingness to suffer, renunciation of desire, the unity of all life-forms, self-purification, self-sacrifice, utter humility, and complete transparency before God. Gandhi captured this Jain heritage in a memorable metaphor, quite typical of his often hyperbolic speech – "I want to reduce myself to zero." Selflessness for Gandhi meant complete freedom of soul and mind as well as the body. It was axiomatic for Gandhi that the *Satyagrahi* would understand that the new vow of nonviolence meant as much self-purification as he could muster.[27] So this way of life, this fundamentally religious vision that was *Ahimsa*, was impossible without the vows of fasting, nonviolence, celibacy, and Truth. They were unthinkable apart from dependence on God and were indispensable qualifications for the *Satyagrahi*. This is why he did not believe socialists and communists would make good *Satyagrahis*. "For a *Satyagrahi* has no stay but God … He may be a passive resister and non-cooperator and so on, but not a *Satyagrahi*."[28] Gandhi was quick to note that he did not intend to tell anyone what God to believe in, although he hoped it would be a God of Truth and Nonviolence. It was his experience that a *Satyagrahi* needed a Supreme Being or Power from whom to draw strength and inspiration. Furthermore, the practical results of such a belief in God were to protect us from self-righteousness, on the one hand, and always to be under God's judgment, on the other.

Part and parcel of this principle of renunciation is the place of suffering in the life of the devotee of *Ahimsa*. "Suffering is the law of human beings; war is the law of the jungle."[29] In South Africa, Gandhi learned that the Eternal Law of Suffering was not only the remedy for undoing wrong and injustice, but was also the Law of Nonviolence. "You have to be prepared to suffer cheerfully at the hands of all and sundry, and you will wish ill to no one, not even to those who may have wronged you."[30]   For Gandhi, as with Christianity, authentic suffering and martyrdom were not sought to bring attention to the sufferer; that would be pathological and self-aggrandizing, if not heretical. For Gandhi and later for King, genuine suffering was always redemptive. It could make all things new. So suffering was a witness to and a sign of the Truth.

Gandhi invoked the example of Jesus, the latter's self-suffering and redemptive sacrifice, to underscore his undying faith in nonviolence. "Jesus lived and died in vain, if he did not teach us to regulate the whole of life by the eternal Law of Love."[31]   In summary, while not being sectarian, dogmatic, or narrowly theological, Gandhi viewed *Ahimsa* as based on what we could, with some safety and accuracy, call a religious foundation and mystical vision with all the attendant moral virtues and spiritual disciplines.

GANDHI'S CAVEATS

No one has more systematically and thoroughly investigated the source, practice, and outcome of nonviolence than the "little brown man from India." Martin Luther King Jr. did not have the time, both in terms of energy and length of years, to probe the depths of this "science". But as we have noted, Gandhi effectively united a dialectic of firm convictions (certainty, confidence) with scientific experimentation (tentativeness, modesty). His introduction to his autobiography states it well. "Far be it from me to claim any degree of perfection for these experiments. I claim for them nothing more than does a scientist who, though he conducts his experiments with the utmost accuracy, forethought, and minuteness, never claims any finality about his conclusion, but keeps an open mind regarding them."[32]

There is no question that Gandhi felt Ahimsa could be used most of the time and that human and divine nature were on its side. But it is significant that he saw reasonable exceptions to the general rule of *Ahimsa*. We have already mentioned his preference for violence over cowardice if they were the only choices we had to make. He immediately dismisses the "violence" of surgeons who cause necessary pain with our consent, of one who destroys rabid dogs who are a menace to humans, and even the social revolutionary who murders and robs for the benefit of the greater society.[33]

Perhaps the most revealing of these exceptions is a chat he had with his son and the story of the wild man in a village. First the conversation with his son: "Thus when my eldest son asked me what he should have done, had he been present when I was almost fatally assaulted in 1908, whether he should have used physical force which he could and wanted to use, and defended me, I told him that it was his duty to defend me even by using violence. Hence it was that I took part in the Boer War, the so-called Zulu rebellion, and the late war. Hence also do I advocate training in arms for those who believe in the method of violence."[34] These are hardly the words of a purist or one who seeks by fiat to universalize his version and practices of nonviolence.

Secondly, the reference to the wild man in a village. "Taking life may be a duty. We do destroy as much life as we think necessary for sustaining our body. Thus for food we take life, vegetable and others, and for health we destroy mosquitoes and the like by the use of disinfectants, etc., and we do not think that we are guilty of irreligion in doing so ... for the benefit of the species, we kill carnivorous beasts ... Even man-slaughter may be necessary in certain cases. Suppose a man runs amuck and goes furiously about, sword in hand, and killing any one that comes in his way, and no one dares to capture him alive. Anyone who dispatches this lunatic will earn the gratitude of the community and be regarded as a benevolent man."[35]

APPROXIMATIONS OF AHIMSA

It is important not to place *ahimsa* up on a pedestal where it is seen as unattainable, or restrict discussion of it to classical texts and examples. In the previous chapter, we gave examples of "approximate *agape*" in contexts chosen for their off-the-pedestal qualities. Here we look at examples of "approximate *ahimsa*."

NONVIOLENCE IN SCHOOLS

One form that education for nonviolence takes in high schools is conflict resolution and peer mediation. Sometimes the programs are referred to as conflict management or peace-building. Philip J. Harack writes about this in G. Simon Harak's *Nonviolence for the Third Millennium*. He is impressed how brutal the impact of insulting remarks are on students, and how violating racial epithets, sexual ridicule, taunting about lack of manhood, are for the mental and physical health of students who are purveyors as well as recipients of this verbal abuse.

The primary assumption on which the nonviolent training is based is that contrary to much of received tradition (religious and secular), human beings are essentially peaceful, and learning to manage conflict is part of learning to be who we really are. Harak invokes "The Seville Statement on Violence" (October, 1990) which noted that twenty international scholars dispelled several myths about violence and human genetics, showing that humans are not genetically predisposed to violence and war.[36]

Confident in this assumption, Harak is assured that conflict can be managed, if not significantly reduced, by nonviolent training in the form of mediation skills. "Mediators are taught that there are specific techniques that help create agreements between our disputants, and in every mediation. The six steps are: (1) the voluntary, agreed upon establishment of the ground rules; (2) the telling of the stories and identifying and defining the problem; (3) identifying underlying issues and feelings; (4) generating options for solutions; (5) writing out and signing the formal agreement; (6) closure, with follow-up by coordinator and disputants' agreement to return if mediation is unsuccessful in practice."[37]

GANDHI'S HIMALAYAN MISCALCULATION

I include this example because Gandhi felt that honest admission of failure was essential for the success of nonviolence. Of course, a Himalayan miscalculation is a very big mistake! The error Gandhi made in the Kheda district was to launch a civil disobedience campaign without adequately preparing his followers in the necessary discipline required for such resistance. "For I have always held that it is only when one sees one's own mistakes with a convex lens, and does just the reverse in the case of others, that one is able to arrive at a just relative estimate of the two. I further believe that scrupulous and conscientious observance of this rule is necessary for one who wants to be a *Satyagrahi*."[38]

For many, this mistake would not have the grand proportions given it by Gandhi, but his conscience dictated such a confession and he further learned, as usual, from his mistake. He would never again prematurely invite people to enter civil disobedience without proper instruction and discipline.

A MODEL PRISONER

Gandhi often referred to jails as temples, and delighted in his many arrests. Echoing Thoreau, he said when a society imprisons a person unjustly, the only place for a just person is in prison. The difference between prisoners who are in jail for doing the right and those who are incarcerated for doing the wrong, is that the latter will not submit willingly to rules of the warden and would escape if it were possible. For Gandhi, the *Satyagrahi* will conform willingly to jail discipline and cooperate in every way with the prison rules. "We have observed that the most distinguished among the prisoners are of greater service inside jails than outside. The coefficient of service is raised to the extent of the strictness with which jail discipline is observed. It is (in jail), therefore, that a civil resister's resistance ceases and his obedience is resumed as soon as he is under confinement. In confinement he claims no privileges because of the civility of his disobedience. Inside the jail by his exemplary conduct he reforms even the criminals surrounding him; he softens the hearts of jailors and others in authority." This behavior related to another of Gandhi's concerns, namely that "every Englishman and English woman must feel safe, not by reason of the bayonet at their disposal, but by reason of our living creed of nonviolence."[39]

One cannot help being reminded of the friendly relationships which developed between judges and the Berrigan brothers, Martin Luther King Jr. to a lesser degree, and others who are dedicated to the discipline of civil disobedience and who proudly and willingly go to jail for principled reasons.

ENGAGED BUDDHISM: THICH NHAT HANH

Thomas Merton wrote about this new Buddhism in his foreword to Thich Nhat Hanh's *Vietnam: Lotus in a Sea of Fire*.[40] The Trappist monk saw the Buddhist monk's activism as a natural expression of his religious tradition. In a real way, although Merton was a cloistered Cistercian and Hanh a political activist, they were soul brothers. These Buddhists were not, Merton said, "immersed in an eternal trance." Withdrawal from a world of suffering and revolution was alien to them. I am reminded of the *bodhisattvas* who refuse the escape from cycles of birth and death, which they have earned and which Nirvana provides, and choose to return to earth again and again until every form of life, from human to animal to every blade of grass, is saved.

An example of this search for the peaceable kingdom is Thich Nhat Hanh's defense of Buddhist monks' self-immolation during the Vietnam War. This defense was included in a letter to Martin Luther King Jr., who was soon to nominate Thich Nhat Hanh for the Nobel Peace Prize. Hanh stressed that the Buddhist monk was not committing suicide. The aim was "at alarming, at moving the hearts of the oppressors, and at calling the attention of the world to the suffering endured then by the Vietnamese. To burn oneself by fire is to prove that what one is saying is of utmost importance ... The importance is not to take one's life, but to burn. What he really aims at is the expression of his will and determination, not death. In the Buddhist belief, life is not confined to a period of 60 or 80 or 100 years; life is eternal. Life is not confined to this body; life is universal. To express will by burning oneself, therefore, is not to commit an act of destruction but to perform an act of construction, that is, to suffer and die for the sake of one's people."

Thich Nhat Hanh saw the direct relation between religious and spiritual profession and social and economic life. He encouraged Martin Luther King, Jr. by saying "You cannot be silent since you have already been in action and you are in action because, in you, God is in action, too." He concluded the letter with a prayer one of his students wrote: "Lord Buddha, help us to be alert to realize that we are not victims of each other. We are victims of our own ignorance and the ignorance of others. Help us to avoid engaging ourselves more in mutual slaughter because of the will of others in power and to predominance."

The Temple Road in Vykom:
Spring 1924 to Autumn 1925

Untouchables were prohibited from using roadways which went past the temple in the Indian village of Vykom. It was of considerable inconvenience for them because it meant a long detour to reach their destination on the other side of the community. Gandhi was always clear about the "Truth" of a campaign and the short- and long-range goals it had in view. The "Truth" here was that every citizen should have access to public roads. The short-term goal was the removal of this prohibition in Vykom and the long-term goal was the eradication of untouchability from India.

Gandhi insisted, since it was a Hindu issue, that local Hindus be active in the leadership of the campaign and that Christians not participate. This was to give integrity to the reformation of the village and not present an offense to orthodox Hindus. After instruction in *Satyagraha* and prayer meetings in the ashram, untouchables joined caste Hindus in nonviolent resistance. Many were beaten, arrested, and jailed. Soon a barricade was erected on the road and the resisters joined positions opposite the police who guarded the wall each day.

When the monsoons came and flooded the road, police occupied their positions in boats. In spite of the water, *Satyagrahis* continued their resistance and stood in three-hour shifts, often in water up to their shoulders. Gandhi arrived and persuaded the authorities to remove the barricade, but the *Satyagrahis* refused to take advantage of this and would not enter the road even though the barrier and police were no longer there. They wanted the village government to declare that untouchables could walk that road. This threw the adversaries off balance and the Brahmins finally succumbed with these words: "We cannot any longer resist the prayers that have been made to us, and we are ready to receive the untouchables."[41] The Vykom campaign is a typical illustration of how Gandhi dealt with Indian injustice. The more familiar (to Westerners) Salt March in 1930 (see Chapter 5), is a parallel example of Gandhi's approach to the international injustice of British exploitation and his nonviolent pursuit of *Swaraj*, independence from Great Britain.

Economic Justice and Nonviolence

Gandhi had two fundamental goals: *Swaraj*, just mentioned, and *Swadeshi*, economic self-support for Indians. He, along with other exploited people, highlighted the importance of the foundation of the human pyramid which Marx and Maslow have made popular. We need food, clothing, and shelter for basic survival. Four years before his death, Gandhi wrote about what, to a great degree, the twentieth century was about:

"Economic equality is the master key to nonviolent independence. Working for economic equality means abolishing the eternal conflict between capital and labor. It means the leveling down of the few rich in whose hands is concentrated the bulk of the nation's wealth on the one hand, and a leveling up of the semi-starved naked millions on the other. A nonviolent system of government is clearly an impossibility so long as the wide gulf between the rich and the hungry millions persists. The contrast between the palaces of New Delhi and the miserable hovels of the poor, laboring class cannot last one day in a free India in which the poor will enjoy the same power as the richest in the land. A violent and bloody revolution is a certainty one day unless there is a voluntary abdication of riches and the power that riches give, and sharing them for the common good."[42]

Notes

1. Eliade, Mircea, <u>Patanjali and Yoga</u>, NY, Schocken Books, 1975, pg. 63.

2. Although Jainism emphasizes Ahimsa as its greatest virtue, warfare and militarism were legitimized and accepted by many Jains and most Indians. Cf. Christianity's history of sponsoring wars, crusades, and its wrestling with the theory of a just war, while proclaiming as its core message, "peace on earth and good will toward all". What Ronald Goetz has said of Christians might also be applied to Jainism. "Whenever Christians engage in coercion in the name of their faith and dogma, their actions somehow seem more reprehensible than those of other people doing the same thing. Christians should realize that whenever they engage in violence in the name of the persecuted Christ, they directly deny Christ. The world has every right to expect and to demand that Christians, who talk as good a love game as anyone, act in a manner consistent with their rhetoric. This is why anti-Christians get so much mileage out of the long history of Christian violence against its foes or its 'heretics'." (<u>Christian Century</u>, July 16-23, 1997, pg. 653.)

3. This version of the vows is from Van Voorst, Robert E., <u>Anthology of World Scriptures</u>, Belmont CA, 1994, pg. 115. The commentary, unless otherwise noted, is my own.

4. Gandhi, M., <u>Non-Violent Resistance</u>, NY, Schocken Books, 1968, pp. 41-42.

5. For a more detailed discussion, read Noss, John and David, <u>Man's Religions</u>, 7th Ed., NY MacMillan, 1989, pp. 99-107.

6. Ferguson, John, <u>War and Peace in the World's Religions</u>, NY, Oxford University Press, 1978, pg. 34.

7. Huston Smith interprets these aspects of Buddhism very well in <u>The World's Religions</u>, San Francisco, Harper, 1991, pp. 99-112.

8. This translation is from Lal, P., <u>Bhagavad Gita</u>, Calcutta, Writers Workshops, 1965.

9. Gandhi, M., The Law of Love, edited by Anand T. Hingori, Bombay, Gharatji Vidya, Bhavan, 1062, pg. 1. (Hereafter referred to as LL). To support this thesis further, Gandhi said "Truth, harmony, brotherhood, and justice are attributes of Ahimsa." LL pg 7.

10. LL, pg. 3. Also "Ahimsa is a science. The word 'failure' has no place in the vocabulary of science. Failure to obtain the expected result is often the precursor to further discoveries." LL, pg. 81.

11. He often refers to "God" in his prayers and conversations. Although Isvara, a word for a personal dimension of Brahman, was available to Gandhi, some say his use of "God" was a way to help westerners gain access to his spiritual discourse. He interchangeably used Hindu and Christian concepts of the supreme Being and it is Gandhi, himself, who sees love, Ahimsa, nonviolence, and Truth as compatible terms. One even sees this compatibility in indices of books about Gandhi. See Chatterjee, Margaret, Gandhi's Religious Thought, Notre Dame, Indiana, University of Notre Dame Press, 1983 and Ashe, Geoffrey, Gandhi, NY, Stein and Day, 1972.

12. Non-Violent Resistance, op. cit., pg. 21.

13. LL, pg. 70.

14. Quoted in Bondurant, Joan, The Conquest of Violence: The Gandhi Philosophy of Conflict. Los Angeles, University of Berkely, 1967, pg. 19. Remember Arjuna's statement in the Gita: "The untrue never is; The True never isn't; The knower of Truth knows this."

15. See Bondurant, op. cit., pg. 9.

16. Non-Violent Resistance, op. cit., pp. 251-252.

17. LL pg 40. See also "Ahimsa is not merely non-killing. A person who remains smugly satisfied with the non-killing of noxious life, but has not love in his heart for all that lives, will be counted as least in the Kingdom of Heaven." LL pg. 45.

18. Gandhi, M., All Men Are Brothers: Autobiographical Reflections, NY, Continuum 1984, pg. 74.

19. LL pg. 38.

20. Non-Violent Resistance, op. cit., pg. 42.

21. Harak, G. Simon, Ed., Nonviolence for the Third Millenium, Macon, Georgia, Mercer University Press, 2000, pg. 121.

22. LL pg. 14.

23. LL pg. 54.

24. LL pg. 55. See also LL pp. 55, 56, 58, 93-94 and All Men are Brothers, op. cit., pp 92-97.

25. Non-Violent Resistance, op. cit., pg. 52.

26. Ibid., pg. 132. The "but" is a crucial qualifier and points to the "Third way" referred to in the title of this chapter.

27. One extreme was the nude itinerant Jain monks who wandered through the countryside begging for their daily sustenance and lodging. They were a threat to no one or thing. Since they were so completely detached from their bodies, all felt safe in their presence.

28. Non-Violent Resistance, op. cit., pg 364. See also NVR pp. 95, 189, and 252.

29. All Men Are Brothers, op. cit., pg. 82.

30. LL pp. 63-64.

31. LL pg. 79.

32. Gandhi, M., Autobiography: The Story of My Experiments with Truth, Boston, Beacon Press, 1969, pg. xiii.

33. LL pg. 37. See also pp. 39-40.

34. Non-Violent Resistance, op. cit., pg. 132.

35. All Men are Brothers, op. cit., pp. 83-84. One wonders why Gandhi did not consider Hitler, whom he thought could be converted by dedicated Satyagrahis, a lunatic running amuck in Europe. For Gandhi's reflections on this see NVR pg. 348ff.

36. <u>Nonviolence for the Third Millenium</u>, op. cit., pg. 186.

37. <u>Ibid</u>. pg. 188.

38. <u>Autobiography</u>, op. cit., pg. 462.

39. <u>Non-Violent Resistance</u>, op. cit., pg. 56.

40. NY, Hill and Wang, 1967. The quotations here are from pp. 106-107.

41. For a complete schedule of and rationale for this event, see Bondurant, pp. 46-52.

42. <u>All Men are Brothers</u>, op. cit., pg. 120. Vinoba Bhave (1885-1982), an Indian disciple of Gandhi's and widely accepted as his spiritual successor, founded the Bhoodan (Land Gift) Movement in 1951. The theme of the movement was an intentional spiritual/socio-economic program called Sarvodaya (the uplift or welfare of all). Bhave and his followers walked from village to village and asked for real estate to be distributed to the landless poor. Although its success was problematic, Bhoodan did help more people than any government sponsored land reform program.

CHAPTER 4

Agape and Ahimsa in Practice

Ira G. Zepp, Jr.

Ideals such as Agape and Ahimsa are very fragile in the rough and tumble of historical and deep-seated conflicts. By virtue of any attempt to practice them, they are refracted and distorted and any such expression emerges as an *approximation* of the ideal. Gandhi tacitly admits as much in response to a criticism leveled at him from time to time, namely, that he was more a politician than a saint. He quickly dispatches the sainthood issue as one would expect, but does suggest that while his decisions were never primarily political, his participation in politics was "because politics encircle us today like the coils of a snake from which one cannot get rid, no matter how much one tries." Gandhi decided, on balance, that it was worthwhile to "wrestle with the snake," to place the purity of religious ideals at risk, in order to achieve a measure of freedom and justice for his people.[1]   Inevitably, a person must live in their own time and in their own locality. A principled politician is faced with the need to work within these boundaries while finding ways to practice values that transcend temporal and geographical limitations. Gandhi knew that wrestling with the snake automatically meant compromising in the arena of strategy and tactics, while at the same time holding tenaciously to his principles of Truth and Ahimsa.

None other than Reinhold Niebuhr, the "realistic" Christian theologian, whose early pacifism was nullified by the unspeakable atrocities of World War I and what he called the sentimental liberal view of evil, saw this same combination of high values and down-to-earth tactics in Martin Luther

King Jr. In a letter to one of us (IGZ) on September 2, 1969, Niebuhr lauded King for his nonviolent resistance to evil as a "real contribution to our civil, moral, and political life … my enthusiasm for Dr. King's nonviolence despite my anti-pacifism was due to my distinction between a pacifism designed to prove our purity and a pacifism designed to establish justice. I thought Dr. King leading a ten percent Negro minority was a good combination of idealism and of pragmatic realism."

King himself often complained about the "paralysis of analysis" and the quietism produced by strict adherence to ideological purity; both could stall, if not prevent, any movement to change oppressive structures. His Birmingham Jail letter was a response to precisely such an issue. King's actions during the 1963 campaign in that city were criticized by several Birmingham clergy as "unwise and untimely." The answer from jail was that time is never neutral; it either works for you or against you. King knew that time is always on the side of the powerful, so there is hardly a "right time" to wrest power from the privileged even if it is done in a nonviolent manner. So, in spite of the fact that a particular time may not be totally appropriate, that not everything can be done, that there will be rough edges to all our activity, and notwithstanding that nonviolent aspirations are delicate and fragile, King in essence said that we ought to aim as high as we can, and not be throttled by the possibility of failure to meet the ultimate goal nor be stymied by fear of adversaries who are ready to question our motives and purity.

Psychologists also tell us that a person's level of aspiration is a major determinant of their eventual level of achievement. So, practically speaking, the higher we aim in terms of Agape and Ahimsa, the greater the amount of justice we will achieve. This principle is more than "pie in the sky." It is very reasonable to believe that if Agape and Ahimsa are our means and goals, any effort on our part to use them and to attain them will be worthwhile, as fractured as our attempts may be. There may be absolutes, King and Gandhi would agree, but they also knew that we do not know them absolutely nor are we able to act on them in any absolute fashion. This is what Reinhold Niebuhr meant by the "relevance of an impossible ideal."

PRESUMPTION OF THE UNITY OF ALL LIFE

Gandhi, as a true Hindu, saw the entire creation connected by the Brahman – Atman unity in all things. Life was unified because of the continuity of divinity which flowed from Brahman through all that exists. As rays are extensions of the sun and qualitatively the same reality as the sun, so is our relationship to God. Or, to use a Hindu metaphor Gandhi preferred, we are to Brahman as drops of water are to the ocean. "We may not be God," said Gandhi, "but we are of God as a drop of water is of the ocean."[2] A drop would shrivel up if taken from the ocean just as we would be extinguished if separated from Brahman.

Underlying Ahimsa is the continuity and unity of all life. "The error of one cannot but affect all and hence man cannot be wholly free from Himsa, from the possibility, however so slightly, of injuring each other."[3] By the same token, any good we do has a rippling effect on all reality.

Since we are linked in total kinship to the Universal Soul, the developmental task expected of human beings is to realize as fully as possible the Atman within them, to become more fully who they are, that is, God-like. It is for this reason that Gandhi never lost faith in humanity in spite of its mistakes; people never lost their sense of capacity, their latent desire to do good. And it is because of this linkage of all life that Gandhi felt Ahimsa could be universalized.

Martin Luther King's Agape was predicated on a proposition

very similar to Gandhi's conviction about the interrelatedness of all life. Integral to his understanding of community, our brother- and sisterhood under God created by agape, was his belief in the "solidarity of the human family."

King saw religious and human life not as a Robinson Crusoe adventure, nor a Lone Ranger flight of solo piety, but as necessarily a communal interpersonal fabric of relationships. The Black church further reinforced this vision with its understanding of the interdependence of oppressed people and that mutual support was a necessary survival skill. King early learned this lesson and later preached and practiced it.

He did not need a radar set to detect that "whatever affects one directly affects all indirectly" and that "the presence of injustice anywhere is a threat to justice everywhere." King's normative statements, found in numerous sermons from his Dexter Avenue and Ebenezer Baptist pulpits, are worth repeating. They are found in, among other places, his last published book, *Trumpet of Conscience*, containing the Massey Lectures he delivered in November and December of 1967 over the Canadian Broadcasting system. "It really boils down to this: that all life is interrelated. We are all caught in an inescapable network of mutuality, tied into a single garment of destiny. We are made to live together because of the interrelated structure of reality."[4] For an addendum to this passage, King always invoked the words of John Donne to shore up his argument about the impossibility of our living isolated lives: "No man is an island, entire unto himself. We are all part of the continent."

The Positive View of Human Nature

As one can readily see from the foregoing discussion, Gandhi believed, and King to a lesser degree, that human nature was not depraved, completely separated from God, nor originally sinful. The Mahatma's understanding of and faith in Ahimsa was based on his positive view of human nature founded on the Brahman-Atman unity mentioned above. Because of this, Gandhi held that if we truly desired it, we could practice the Law of Love, which was in accord with our humanity. This is why Gandhi concluded that nonviolence is more natural for us than violence.

If humanity is threaded by divinity we are basically good and can do the good. This fueled Gandhi's confidence that nonviolence could be learned by everyone, not just sadhus, swamis, and monks. It is not a cloistered virtue, but one "applicable as much in the (cloister) and legislature as in the market place."[5]

A striking example of his faith in this method is Gandhi's rather lengthy, finely nuanced response to a question about how to deal with a thief in your house. The question asked him was, "Why should we not obtain our goal, which is good, by any means possible?" Gandhi's response was in essence "It all depends. A response would be different if it were your father, simply an acquaintance, a stranger, an Englishman, an Indian, or whether the thief was strong or weak."

If the thief were armed, that's another story. In that case, Gandhi said, "I would simply remain quiet. If the robber persists with the neighbor or yourself, you realize he is an ignorant brother, a fellow man, and that stealing is a disease with him. So keep your doors and windows open and keep your things most accessible to him. This will confuse the robber and throw him off balance. His mind will become agitated after learning of your broad and loving heart. He will repent, beg your pardon, return your things and refrain from stealing."[6] As "out of sync" as we are with this sort of response to violence, Gandhi really counted on this happening in the majority of cases because of his faith in people. To say the least, it is a viewpoint that can stimulate lively debate.

The young Martin Luther King had a liberal perspective on human nature, if for no other reason than that he was a member of an oppressed group. People in bondage and without privilege cannot afford the conceit and luxury of seeing human beings as damned sinners, depraved, and incapable of virtue. They know better. Furthermore, it is too debilitating, too despairing. King's various versions of "Pilgrimage to Nonviolence" reveal his devotion to liberalism, rational truth and an appreciation of the possibility of human beings to be better by their own will power. King knew, with most successful leaders and revolutionaries, that social change occurs as a result of hope in human possibility and that the achievement of justice is not motivated but hampered by despair over the limitations of one's ability.

In addition, King as an intellectual liberal, owed much to his graduate training and to the sermons of such black preachers as Benjamin Mays and Vernon Johns and such white preachers as Harry Emerson Fosdick, Ernest Freemont Tittle, and J. Wallace Hamilton. All these men were notable pulpiteers in the mid-twentieth century and dominated the thinking of many mainstream black and white clergy and other church leaders.[7]

Most of King's sermons in *Strength to Love* abound with these progressive references, especially to the "Fatherhood of God and Brotherhood of Man", a virtual mantra of this liberal tradition. If Jesus said, "Love your enemies," King and the other proponents of this tradition believed that Jesus was not mocking us; rather, he believed it was within our power to love our enemies, and that it was vitally important to do so.

To be sure, the later King was profoundly influenced by Reinhold Niebuhr's qualification of the simple love ethic of Jesus espoused by liberal theologians. Although he saw some of Niebuhr's "realistic" thought about human nature exemplified by the recalcitrance of northern ghettos, a serious case can be made that this dialogue with Niebuhr was primarily an intellectual exercise; in reality King never lost his faith in nonviolence and thus, in the goodness and capacity of human beings.

Both Gandhi and King depended on tapping the consciences of people, made vulnerable and receptive by their humanist and religious traditions, to respond eventually in a positive way to the persistent, well-intended dedication of nonviolent protesters. Jan Smuts of South Africa said of Gandhi's strategy there, "You have reduced me to helplessness." After Gandhi's Salt March, English police were so impressed with the courage and endurance of the Satyagrahis that one was forced to admit, "You can't hit a bugger when he stands up to you like that" and upon giving him a mock salute, walked away. And recall how the fire hoses of Birmingham police fell limp in the presence of the sincerity and bravery of the practitioners of King's nonviolent civil-disobedience in that thought-to-be-impenetrable southern bastion of segregation.

In all fairness, these might be considered anecdotal occurrences, insufficient to make a strong case for nonviolence. They are rare indeed, but what happened once can happen again. Gandhi and King would say that these nonviolent "exceptions" prove the rule of the effectiveness of nonviolence to produce genuine personal and social change. If we are now just at the beginning of a shift toward a more nonviolent paradigm, the importance of these examples is not diminished by their rarity. Rather, these examples of successful nonviolence are like "existence proofs" in logic or mathematics; they establish that new ways of doing things are possible.

LITTLE'S NONVIOLENT REVOLUTIONARY TOLERANCE

David Little, Professor of the Practice in Religion, Ethnicity, and International Conflict at Harvard Divinity School, has written a brilliant and insightful essay entitled "Coming to Terms with Religious Militancy." The essay is essentially a typology of violence and tolerance. His major categories are: Revolutionary Intolerance (Violent), Revolutionary Tolerance (Violent), Revolutionary Tolerance (Nonviolent), Civic Intolerance, and Civic Tolerance.

Of special interest to us is his sub-section on Revolutionary Tolerance achieved by nonviolence. There would be no more appropriate summary and conclusion to this part of the book than to quote some excerpts from Professor Little's article.

"Jesus, Gandhi, Martin Luther King Jr., and contemporaries like the Dalai Lama, the Cambodian Buddhist monk Maha Gosananda and the Mennonite peace theorist-activist John Paul Lederach are all examples of religious militants who seek a radical transformation of policies, practices and institutions, but who do so in the spirit of nonviolence. They are militant because they envision their missions as an uncompromising battle against the forces of evil and injustice. They are nonviolent because they all believe that the ultimate enemy is violence itself, and that the way to combat it is to absorb and sublimate it, rather than to practice it. The true enemy – the threat to all that is holy and good – is the temptation to give in to violence, and that may be resisted only by practicing nonviolence. The implied commitment includes forswearing all forms of force, not just those that are extra-legal or unrestrained and indiscriminate. Any direct use of force is a step toward violence. At the same time coercion, understood as the act of withholding benefits, is often acceptable... However resolute in disapproving evil and injustice, one must always endure or bear with it, at least in the sense of not responding with force. One may, of course, employ nonviolent means of resistance.

"Nonviolent tolerant militancy also expands our understanding of tolerance. According to the Dalai Lama, tolerance 'can be learned only from one's enemy – it cannot be learned from your guru.' Occasions of conflict may be turned to advantage by regarding them as opportunities for mastering the distress and frustration normally associated with disagreement and dispute. One learns to welcome conflict in order to strengthen self-restraint, as well as to clarify and deepen conviction."[8]

ARE AGAPE AND AHIMSA REALIZABLE?

A nonviolent view of life includes three perspectives, discussed briefly in this chapter, that a person might not associate immediately with the word nonviolence, or with its roots, agape and ahimsa. First is the idea that approximations of these ideals are acceptable. Second is the view of the world as being interconnected in a complex way; this means that our efforts matter and are not isolated. Third is the positive view of human nature, which gives hope and also motivates us toward caring and away from violence. All three of these ideas are supportable not only by faith but by rigorous argument and empirical observation. They strengthen the conjecture that agape and ahimsa are realizable, and bring nonviolence down to earth where it can walk on the ground a little.

Notes

1. <u>Non-Violent Resistance</u>, op. cit., pg. 109.

2. <u>LL</u> pg. 66. It is instructive to note that, for traditional Christianity, agape is a derivative value, that is, we do not have it by virtue of birth. It is bestowed by God. Ahimsa, on the other hand, is an inherent value by way of our being extensions of Brahman.

3. <u>LL</u> pg. 35.

4. King, Martin Luther, Jr., <u>Trumpet of Conscience</u>, NY, Harper and Row, 1968, pg. 69.

5. LL pg. 99. Many critics consider this naïve, romantic, and optimistic view of humanity the Achilles heel of nonviolent movements. The Hitler card is often played; Gandhi thought Hitler could be converted by true Satyagrahis and Dietrich Bonhoeffer, once an ardent pacifist, was a member of a team who planned to assassinate Hitler. Bonhoeffer said "There are some things worse than violence and that is tyranny." As we discussed earlier in this chapter, there are few doctrinaire nonviolent resisters.

6. Nonviolent Resistance, op. cit., pp. 12-14 and 350-352.

7. For an excellent discussion of how dependent King was on these liberal resources, see Miller, Keith D., Voice of Deliverance: The Language of Martin Luther King Jr. and its Sources, NY, The Free Press (Macmillan), 1992.

8. Harvard Divinity Bulletin, Volume 29, No. 1, 2000 pg. 19.

Part II

Outcomes:
Nonviolence Education and
its Effects on People

In Part I, we explored the origins of nonviolence through an examination of *agape* and *ahimsa*. In Part II, we will look at nonviolence as a teachable discipline made up of ideas and skills, and do so in a way that is at least partly empirical.

Chapter 5 presents reactions of students to video documentaries on two nonviolent movements: the Nashville lunch counter sit-ins of 1960, and Gandhi's 1930 Salt March. Chapter 6 summarizes much of the content from one kind of nonviolence training workshop. Chapter 7 gives an outcome-oriented review of what is learned as a result of studying nonviolence, based on conversations with students who have begun to study nonviolence in courses or have been through a training experience such as Chapter 6 describes. Chapter 8 presents an exchange of correspondence between two people, Ira Zepp and Bill Holmes, which was occasioned by the terrible violence on September 11, 2001. Chapter 9 concludes the book with a discussion of two important issues: measurable outcomes, and applications of nonviolence in threatening situations.

Thus, we examine "outcomes" of nonviolence education through the thoughts and concerns of different kinds of people: students encountering nonviolence for the first time; people who have had a more extensive training experience; individuals possessing many years of experience with these ideas; and tough-minded scientists, law enforcement officers, and others who are faced with daunting "reality demands" as they contemplate applications of nonviolence to their work.

CHAPTER 5

Reactions to Learning about
Two Nonviolent Movements

Charles E. Collyer
and Students of the University of Rhode Island

The student reaction papers in this chapter were written during the Spring of 2002 by students in a General Psychology class at the University of Rhode Island's College of Continuing Education in Providence, RI. The students in this class were diverse in age, racial and ethnic identification, and gender. The course introduced Psychology by presenting five general perspectives on the field, of which one was called the Sociocultural perspective.[1] Within this part of the course, topics such as prejudice and stereotypes, power and social influence, cultural identity, and group processes, were discussed. One morning, the class viewed two segments from the Public Broadcasting series on nonviolence movements, *A Force More Powerful*[2], and students were asked to write a short reaction paper on what they had seen. The two short documentaries were on the 1960 Nashville sit-in movement (in which our colleague and friend Bernard LaFayette Jr. had been one of the student leaders), and on the 1930 Salt March led by Mohandas Gandhi in India. The scope of each documentary will be described first.

THE TWO MOVEMENTS

NASHVILLE, 1960

There are many 20th century nonviolent movements from around the world that are available for study. The one chosen by the producers of *A Force More Powerful* to represent the U.S.

civil rights struggle was the Nashville sit-in campaign of 1960.
The sit-ins in Greenville NC, Nashville TN, and subsequently
other communities, stand as an intermediate phase between
the early events of the civil rights movement such as the
Montgomery bus boycott, and the later campaigns such as
Birmingham and Selma, which changed federal laws. It has
been argued that the Nashville campaign convinced Martin
Luther King Jr. to place renewed emphasis on nonviolent direct
action, and so set the stage for the campaigns of the mid-1960s
which produced the Civil Rights Act of 1964 and the Voting
Rights Act of 1965. David Halberstam has also recounted the
story of the Nashville movement and its impact in some detail
in his book *The Children*.[3]

In the winter of 1959-60, Diane Nash, Bernard LaFayette
Jr., John Lewis, James Bevel, and other students at Nashville
colleges began to attend evening workshops on nonviolence
led by the Rev. James Lawson. Martin Luther King Jr. had
asked Lawson to come south from Ohio to teach Gandhian
methods to young people interested in confronting the Jim
Crow system of legalized segregation. In the workshops,
Lawson's young friends learned about the term *ahimsa*, and
Lawson connected it to the Christian ideal of love, of *agape*.
They discussed the successes of nonviolent campaigns under
Gandhi's leadership in India. They debated how to respond
to threats and intimidation nonviolently, without impulsively
provoking an escalation of violence. They practiced sitting in
rows while their friends role-played white bigots who taunted
and even physically abused them.

The students organized a strategy for desegregating lunch
counters in several downtown department stores, by having
groups of black and some white students sit down together
and order food. They were refused service as a matter of
store policy, because the stores at that time were allowed to

discriminate against black customers. The reaction to the sit-ins progressed from amazed inaction to semi-organized resistance. Groups of young white men did attack the students, as had been anticipated in the workshops. The demonstrators did not retaliate, but were arrested and jailed, while their attackers were not charged. The nonviolent strategy increasingly drew serious national attention to the cause of desegregation, and questioning of Nashville's official stance on what was legally allowed in the city and what was not.

After a bomb blast destroyed the house of Z. Alexander Looby, the students' legal counsel, there was a march to City Hall, which received a high level of media attention. Diane Nash confronted the mayor of Nashville with the question whether it was right for stores to discriminate against some of their customers on the basis of their color. With the cameras running, the mayor declared that it was not right. The process of desegregating the city's businesses and other public facilities began with that declaration.

INDIA, 1930

Mohandas K. Gandhi's career was long and rather complicated. He became known as a proponent and leader of nonviolent social change during his first career as an attorney in South Africa. After returning to his native India in 1915, his second career was devoted to moving India toward independence from British colonial rule. *A Force More Powerful* provides succinct glimpses of the two careers. The introduction to the series begins in a South African jail, and notes not only Gandhi's contribution to the early struggles for human rights in that country, but also his influence on many nonviolent movements of the 20th century which were to follow him. The documentary on the Salt March provides a visually compelling illustration of Gandhi's methods and an overview of the struggle for Indian independence.

In March of 1930 Gandhi, by now a revered nonviolent "saint" throughout much of India, chose the British tax on salt as the target of a direct action campaign. Salt was a relatively minor part of the overall economy of the British Raj, but the impact of the salt tax was felt by everyone, and especially by the very poor. Furthermore, as a symbol of unreasonable exploitation, the salt tax could be understood to represent a much wider array of grievances. The campaign was initiated by marching 240 miles from Ahmedabad to Dandi, on the seacoast, where salt would be made for free in defiance of the British law.

In several ways, the Salt March exemplified Gandhi's approach to noncooperation with an unjust system. It focused on a specific issue, the salt tax, rather than everything at once. It entailed discipline and planning; his core group of marchers were members of his own ashram, who understood nonviolence and the purpose of the demonstration. It was extended over a period of time to allow attention to be drawn to the issue; at about 10 miles per day, it took many days to walk 240 miles. It provided opportunities for many people to participate, even in very simple ways; a person could participate by illegally evaporating sea water to recover the salt.

As the documentary makes clear, the Salt March and other actions of the campaign against the salt tax did not immediately produce a dramatic change in India's status. But they set the stage for later political developments leading to independence, and they provided mythic stories that helped Indians to know their own power and to appreciate nonviolence as an instrument of change. India and Pakistan have had a turbulent history since their independence in 1947 from the old British Raj. However, a feeling of pride in the cultural legacy of Gandhi's nonviolence remains strong; Gandhi now belongs to the world, but his home, and the source of his teaching, was India.

The Reaction Papers

These selections are reactions, not to a full course or workshop on nonviolence, but to less than an hour of exposure to documentary stories that emphasized nonviolent approaches to social change. The views of the students sometimes support the points we have made about nonviolence in other chapters of this book, and sometimes advance contrary ideas or associate the documentaries with other stories and concepts that were meaningful to the individual writers. The reaction papers, from 12 of the 30 students in the class, were selected primarily for their conceptual diversity, and for how clearly the writer's ideas were expressed. We particularly invite readers of this book who are teachers to reflect on this sampling of initial thoughts on nonviolence. We have done only minor editing (principally spelling) of the students' writing; we felt that the flavor and meaning of the original papers came through best if we let them speak for themselves. However, we did add the subtitles.

1. Disbelief

My reaction to these two films is very easy for me to write about. First, I cannot believe that I did not learn about this in high school. I feel like this is an injustice to me. When I left class last Wednesday, I felt like I wanted to know more about these two movements in history. These movements give such an important message to people. Dedication and teamwork can make anything happen!

The Jim Lawson workshops were awesome. The message was so clear that a nonviolent approach actually meant fighting back. Fighting with nonviolence may seem like more of a challenge, but it is the way people are won over. The way they sat-in every Saturday in the diners, even though they were being beaten over it is such an inspiration. They knew that their arrests dramatized their grievances in a positive way, so it was worth every bit of agony for them. They had to deal with a mayor who claimed to uphold the law but supported the storeowners (and men who broke the law by assaulting the students). They were addressing the country and the world with these acts. The progress they made, although it took about three years, was astonishing. Their perseverance is so uplifting. It is good knowing that if something in this world needs to be done, we can do it. We just need to stick together and make people aware.

I was so interested in Mahatma Gandhi. He really was a saint. His way of communicating to the people how and why they were going to be free was very clever. How did he even know that if they made their own salt and clothes, the British would be less powerful? And most importantly, how would one guy get 350 million Indians free from the powerful British government? Because Gandhi was a nonviolent warrior, he won over many people. The government did lose control, because of violence. When police became brutal to Indians, the British civilians began not following the government so strongly. Their violence backfired on them. Although Gandhi was arrested and was eventually assassinated, his work was not in vain. Everything cannot change at once, but Gandhi definitely made something huge happen.

– R. C.

2. Anger

Viewing the film on non-violent demonstrations and peace, my main reaction is anger. I feel as if the Southern blacks did not have a choice. If they had reacted violently the results would have most likely been death, or jail. Blacks were not given the opportunity to express themselves, the laws were designed against them, and they did not have many advocates. To resort to violence would have probably increased the odds against them.

I am trying to understand the thoughts and actions of the Southern white people. The people seemed unaware of the degradation and horror that must have surrounded these people at this time. To put in place laws that did not allow human beings to utilize even the basic necessities like a bathroom, to me is just not rational. To deny children equal education and opportunity is sinful. The action of these people is a clear contradiction of their professed Christianity.

The idea of non-violence appeals to me in this instance, only because it worked. The Southern Blacks achieved what they set out to achieve, but I imagine myself in the same situation and the anger is overwhelming. I feel the Whites should have been beaten and segregated and denied certain rights. I would like to see what the outcome would have been. I do not believe White people would have resorted to a non-violent protest. I do not believe that they would have the staying power that the Blacks demonstrated.

I believe it took intelligence and will for the Blacks to carry out an act of non-violence, but my anger is not allowing me to see the Psychology in what they did. I cannot speak for all people of color, but if I were to guess, I would say that the majority would have reacted to non-violence with violence.

– C. R.

3. The Sympathy of Bystanders

The movie we watched in class was very interesting. The students in Nashville used the same method of nonviolence that Gandhi used to bring attention and change to the society they lived in. This approach of nonviolence was very effective. When Gandhi used this approach to get rid of British rule it made the officers look real evil and mean hearted. The reason is looking at footage of police officers beating people in the street looks terrible because the people are not fighting back. It makes a person wonder "how can somebody beat a man or woman for no reason and the person they are beating is not fighting back?" It makes an observer want to listen to the side of the person who is getting beaten because it makes the other side look like savages. That is why Gandhi received a lot of press from all over, even in America. The same goes for people in the South.

This approach of nonviolence worked when the people in Nashville and the people in India were organized, had a leader, and were consistent. I'm sure if people were not organized with a leader the Indian people wouldn't have gotten their freedom and African-Americans would not have gotten the equality they wanted in the South. If only some people followed the nonviolence approach and others did not, things would not have changed in the British Empire or America because if the people who felt they were being oppressed fought back with fists and guns they would have looked like rebels and it would have made the things they were fighting for really nonexistent. The nonviolence approach is a weapon that affects the way a person or people see a situation and when people in Nashville and all across America saw what was going on it brought about change in the South, and the same goes for India.

Another thing I thought about while watching the movie was the nonviolence approach does not just involve the two oppositions but has a third part which is the observer or observers. An example of this is a real life one. I used to go to Classical High School, and I used to go to Kennedy Plaza to wait for buses with my friends sometimes and there used to be a lot of fights there. One time there was a fight where it was approximately four on five. And the kids were going at it, each one throwing wild punches at each other with yelling and screaming. After the fight was broken up you could hear some people saying things like "Well, there people go again fighting downtown," and "I swear people love fighting in Kennedy Plaza!" Another time I was downtown there was another fight in which two kids got jumped by three kids. The three kids who jumped them were swinging at the two kids hard, but the only thing the two kids did was cover themselves for protection against the blows until the fight was stopped. They did not throw one punch and even after the fight they did not yell in anger, just looked in disbelief. After the fight some people actually went up to the kids to see if they were all right. Now if you compare these two different instances you can see how the nonviolence approach affects people. In the first case, all of the kids were fighting and the people watching were looking at it like "oh well, there's fighting again." In the second case where the two kids who were getting jumped did not fight back, some people came to them to see if they were all right. So in conclusion somehow the nonviolence approach affects people watching the situation, bringing out their compassion and concern about what is going on.

– P. H.

4. CLOSER AND CLOSER TO HOME

Last week in class we watched a movie titled "A Force More Powerful." This film was about nonviolence and how people today and in the past have changed the world through nonviolence. The term nonviolence is defined as the fight to win someone over without using violence. This film held a very powerful message that I think everyone has to think about and apply it in his or her life.

The first historical event using nonviolence was in Nashville, Tennessee, in 1960. A group was formed to try to desegregate the town's lunchrooms and have everyone dine together. They set out on a Saturday morning by having Blacks sit at the diner counters for hours trying to get served. The groups were eventually arrested but had other groups fill in for them directly afterwards. This sent the town into an uproar, no one was injured right away, and eventually it worked.

I thought that during this time in history a challenge like this was very courageous. Though the challenge used nonviolence, the lawyer representing the Black students had his house bombed. It seems like no matter what technique is used violence is always present in some form or another. Though it is awful to say, sometimes it may seem like the only way.

The true inspiration for nonviolence in America was Gandhi, who set out on a nonviolent task thirty years prior to the sit-ins in Tennessee. Gandhi walked to the beaches of India, setting out to make his own salt and not pay tax, emphasizing injustice to the poor. Though these types of historic leaders are practicing civil disobedience they are not physically harming people to get their point across.

Today it seems no one thinks in these terms. I am personally a large supporter of nonviolence and feel anything can get solved by using this technique. Though I can honestly say I experience violence almost day to day. Whether it is seeing a parent scold a child the wrong way, disrespecting peers or witnessing a fight at a bar, it is all around us. I really thought this film showed a positive message that everyone should learn about in large cities and rural areas.

I come from a small town in Western Massachusetts and in high school there were two groups that were always fighting with each other. I'm sure that if they talked it out they would realize they have a lot in common and that words can get distorted and lead to violence. I thought this video offered a lot of positive information and it really made me think about my personal experiences.

– E. T.

5. Unthinking Ways

In the movies that we watched in class the one on Gandhi really opened my eyes about what we as a people need to do to overcome all our fears of other races and religions. If there was a force out there that could make all of the races on earth come together and force them to talk about their differences, this would show all of the people that we can all get along together without violence. This would also show people that everybody has the same fears about others, and finally break down the barrier of ignorance. The movies also showed me that the best way to beat an unfair system is to do it nonviolently. This way they cannot make excuses for beating people up or throwing them in jail. The movie showed me that most people don't even think for themselves, they just do what people tell them to do because they don't know how to think on their own. They didn't stop and think that African-Americans are people too who have feelings. When Diane Nash asked the mayor if it was fair how the African-Americans were being treated, he had to stop and think about that question, and finally he said it was not fair. This is an example of how people don't think about the consequences of their actions because they never had to. The South was run like that for years, and after a few generations it becomes a system that everybody follows blindly.

One of the strong points in the movie was when Gandhi started to walk to the ocean and make salt illegally. He picked up a lot of people on the way that felt the same way he did about their oppressors. They felt this way because they were being taxed on something that they needed; they couldn't get around paying for salt because the Viceroy made all the laws and would have them thrown in jail. This is another example of people not caring for another group of people; the Viceroy didn't think of the Indian people as equals, but as second-class citizens or less. If someone had made the Viceroy think about what he was doing or questioned whether the British were there in India for any good reason, it would have made a lot of difference. Perhaps he would have opened his eyes and questioned the point of treating people unfairly. This brings up the point I stated earlier about most people don't even think for themselves. Stanley Milgram's experiment on obedience is related to this.[4]

- A. S.

6. Bravery and Gratitude

I did not know that Gandhi invented the nonviolence protest tactic. Gandhi's idea was a remarkable beginning to a new era of freedom, not only for his country of India, but for other countries around the world. His protest walk to the salt beach seemed like a small accomplishment at first, but as news of Gandhi's march got around to other communities, more and more people joined his walk for freedom against Great Britain. Regardless of the serious consequences Great Britain placed upon Gandhi and his followers, they continued on with the protest. Gandhi's cause was for the freedom of the Indian people. By believing in this cause Gandhi knew that he might die because of it. For Gandhi this was all worth it. Forty years later Americans did the same thing. Black Americans were tired and upset with the segregation between Blacks and Whites in their community. The African-Americans started the civil rights movement against segregated businesses, schools, and jobs in their communities. I agree 100% with this cause and respect every person who was involved with the civil rights movement. I thank all of these brave heroes for my freedom that I have today.

The death and abuse that the African-American men, women, and children experienced was so sad. To think that people can be so cruel to humans because of their race! Today, America has come a long way from the 1960's, but America still needs repair work when it comes to fairness between races. Dr. Martin Luther King Jr., Gandhi, and other civil rights leaders and protesters, served a great purpose for the freedom that we have in the world today. We as the new generation must continue the nonviolent fight for rights and peace for all races around the world.

– J. R.

7. Perspective

After seeing the two documentaries last week, a lot of things were put into perspective for me. I had no idea how bad things seemed to get back then and also what lengths were gone through to make things change. I completely congratulate every single person involved in the "lunch room sit-ins." What a great idea to make known that no one was going to stop them from getting the respect that was very obviously deserved. Those students who did that must have had some outrageous courage to do just a little of what they did. They had to know that they had the chance of getting beat, hurt, and even possibly killed just to get their points across to everyone else.

Being White, I am ashamed of all the White people who attacked those Black students just for sitting at their "all white counters". Who were they to decide who could and could not sit there? They were not and never would be God, so that was never up to them. Just the fact that those students were arrested for sitting at a counter was horrible in my eyes. What did they do wrong? All they were doing was fighting for the rights that they, as humans, deserved and were not getting. Gandhi was obviously a great inspiration to all of those students as well as to all of the other millions of people who go along with the "nonviolence" idea. I personally think that this should be enforced all the time. Just looking at what happened here proves that though it may take time, it is possible to win battles by using brains over force and brutality. Is that a hard concept to grasp or what? Obviously it must be, because though things have changed a lot, things will never be the way they should be. Every single person in this country, in the world, should have the rights they deserve. Being in the U.S. means a person has rights and shall be treated as an equal. Nowhere in that sentence does it say except for color. We need to enforce that, and not be so mean to people just because they aren't White. Color means nothing, brains mean everything. I really like what Gandhi stood for and believe what he fought for and taught his followers were right.

– A. P.

8. The World is One

Conflict is everywhere. Sixteen year olds are blowing themselves up in the name of God. Countries threaten each other with trade embargoes and increasing oil costs. Everyone wants it her/his way or no way at all and if anyone disagrees they will be conquered or destroyed. We disrespect our environment; we disrespect each other; and we disrespect that which is greater than ourselves. The world has forgotten that it is one and it must be shared. It has forgotten that boundaries and borders are defined because the human race has deemed it so.

The film on nonviolence presented in class last week showed us how influential leaders of the past avoided violence while fueling major social movements. People such as Mohandas Gandhi and Martin Luther King Jr. were not willing to accept the injustices of the world and expressed their discontent through nonviolent action. I believe many people are equally discontented with society in the 21st century as Gandhi and King were in the 20th. Yet we continuously overlook the importance of nonviolent action. People are showing their anger through fighting and nothing is changing except the increasing amount of violence in the world.

Furthermore, we have become so consumed with individual gain that it has created a great deal of isolationism; for it is much easier to stay in one's own little world than to see the world of one's fellow human being. We must cease inconsiderateness and gradually begin to decrease the level of ignorance we have of one another's lifestyles. A small adjustment in an individual's life, such as using public transportation or walking as often as possible, is a nonviolent action that leads to a decrease in oil consumption which then leads to decreasing the power of oil moguls; a slight decrease but a decrease nonetheless.

Nonviolent action is crucial to making us realize that the world is one and it must be shared as equally as humanly possible. Humanity can decrease violent conflict. We just need to show that we care through what we buy, eat, and drive. The world will shift slowly but effectively. Our choices must clarify that we reject violence and no longer fear peace.

– J. P.

9. WORTH FIGHTING FOR

To begin, I have to say that this video on nonviolence truly inspired me. There are not too many people these days that will stand up for what is right in order to make a change. Rather, every day you hear the world complain about what should be done in order to create justice and equality. Personally, I feel as though it takes courage and strength to stand up for what you believe in nonviolently.

While watching the movie I gained a lot of insight about what it's like to be mistreated and underprivileged, but I had never really thought about the strength and power it took to overcome these tribulations. Every day of my life I experience other people's mistreatment and even sometimes my own, and it is the worst feeling in the world to not be able to change it and feel overpowered. However, I no longer complain. I have learned now that action does speak louder than words, so instead I gather my thoughts and spread knowledge among those that are intimidated by authority. The African Americans in Nashville fought for their freedom and American status. They encouraged me to believe that all things are worth fighting for, even the small things. In further thought, the nonsense that goes on at my job allows me to step one foot in the door. For example, a majority of my co-workers feel threatened by the management staff, who abuse their authority to the max. Therefore, I took it upon myself to write a letter to the district manager of the company. But it does not stop there; I am now held accountable to speak on behalf of the staff at the next store meeting.

In conclusion, I now know that the struggle may be long and may unfortunately have no result, but it is worth the defeat. Nobody in this world should have to live their life without dignity, but sadly to say, it happens. More people should realize that life is worth fighting for no matter what the circumstances. However, what we must remember is that you kill evil with kindness, nonviolently. Nothing in this world will ever be equal, but with inspiring people like Gandhi and Diane Nash, the power, strength, and courage is all mine.

- L. O.

10. RESPECT

I hold the utmost degree of respect for the Fisk University students, their supporters concerning the events in Nashville, as well as for Gandhi, his supporters, and their persistent efforts to bring about change through nonviolence. This is truly remarkable, because I feel so few are capable of achieving change by this method. That is, pursuing change in defiance of the status quo and the oppression that accompanies it. It takes quite a unique individual, and furthermore an individual who is part of something much larger, who is one soul joined with the souls of many others in unison to further the movement.

When most people think of nonviolence movements the name Martin Luther King Jr. virtually always comes to mind first, and the 1960s peace marches and sit-ins join those first thoughts. For most, Gandhi's movements are overshadowed by those of the 1960s, yet essentially it all began with Gandhi 30 years earlier and one could say that his policies served as a model for those who were soon to begin in our country. I admire him because he was the first to demonstrate that sacrifices would have to be made for the ultimate betterment of the majority.

In the textbook this is defined as altruism. I do not observe too many practicing this today. The decrease of morally sound individuals and the increase of greedy individuals are in part what our society has come to today. Some may argue that perhaps we see less altruism today because there is less in terms of legal injustices to protest, but I disagree. I feel there is much to be done and I remember it every time I drive down the street and see a police vehicle. Unfortunately, I do not feel that we will ever approach this kind of greatness again. The world is much more violent than it has ever been, and that is reflected in people's refusal to cooperate with one another and in their actions towards one another.

For the type of movement we saw in Nashville in 1960 and for the greater part of the decade was systematic. There was concern that if one or two people lost their nerve and submitted to violence it would have jeopardized the whole thing. It was mentioned in the documentary that this is what their opposition wanted to see happen. They saw it as a passing fad, and thought it would soon go away with arrests, beatings, and other forms of intimidation. Instead it has gone down in history as something much more, because of the exercise of moral discipline and teamwork.

– M. M.

11. Taught Me A Lot

In the PBS special we watched two segments both dealing with nonviolent protest. The first segment dealt with segregation in Tennessee and the second segment was about Gandhi. Both segments taught me a lot about nonviolence.

In the first episode, we watched the segregation in Tennessee. The episode taught all about nonviolent demonstration. The demonstrators used different means other than violence to get their message across to the white members of the community. The black demonstrators first tried to desegregate counters in restaurants. The way they did this was by using three groups of people that came in, one group after the other groups were arrested. The second episode was about Gandhi and how he marched members of his movement to the sea. While watching Gandhi I did not really agree with him, because all he did was march and collect different members throughout the communities. I did agree with how he asked different members of the government to step down from their positions. I did agree with this because it breaks down the chain of command.

Before I watched this movie the only kind of demonstration I was used to was the violent type. I have watched on television the L.A. riots as well as many other ones. I never realized that it could be done in a nonviolent way. By watching these segments it showed me that more is accomplished from nonviolence than violence. Not as many people die, and people get their message across more effectively by not hurting anyone. This really shows me that they stand for what they believe in.

– J. H.

12. WHAT IS "NORMAL"?

While watching these videos in class, I can feel myself wishing it were more like this everywhere. It can be hard for some to relate to this nonviolent method of bringing changes to the world. I would guess this goes back as far as when we were children. The *Tough Guise*[5] issue would also apply here. If we were not taught to fight with weapons and violence, if it were not "normal", how different things might be in the world. I once told my husband that if we were involved in a war, I would take my grandson far away so he would never have to kill another person or be killed himself. My husband was very upset by this and I really do understand why. He went into the Army right out of high school and made a career of it. He truly believes a man should fight for his country and protect his family. I too believe this, yet I pray for a different answer or a different method. People do what they feel to be normal or what they are taught to be right. He was raised to think this way like many men. How do we change this type of thinking?

In watching, I came to the conclusion that it took more bravery for those people to stand tough with no violence or weapons than it took for any of the officials with their clubs and guns at their sides. People who use force as a means to settle something are not using their God-given gift of thought. I realize these men are being given orders to use force, but this does not make it all right. Here is an example of Milgram's obedience study where we follow orders, especially from people of a higher status, and follow these orders no matter who we hurt. We can also see Zimbardo's study[6] is evident in how things can get carried away when a little power is involved. Fear is also a big factor in how we react to a situation. We may be more forceful if we are more frightened.

People who use force and follow orders are only doing what is natural in this day and age. It is what we see all around us in every aspect of our life. If we started with our children in schools and showed them other ways to solve issues and ways of nonviolence, we may have a chance to change our current beliefs. Maybe if we showed both sides of an issue and how we have dealt with it in the past, children would see the nonviolent way as a better method. It is very hard to look at both sides of an issue when only one side is visible. I do not recall ever seeing one thing about nonviolent methods in all my years in school. This is the first time I have actually become aware of it. I had heard of Martin Luther King, Jr. and Gandhi but never really knew what they represented. Hopefully in our future years our children and their children will find a more peaceful way to communicate and discuss matters of the world.

– E. H.

Thoughts on the Reaction Papers

There are some themes in the students' writing that teachers of nonviolence will probably recognize. First, the students saw the relevance of nonviolence to core human concerns. There is eloquence in the way many people expressed their feelings about these core concerns. There is an acknowledged lack of past education and information about nonviolence. There is amazement and disbelief that such important material would be withheld from children and from people generally. There are emotions such as anger, evoked by the oppression which nonviolence has often opposed. There are insights derived, such as the idea that what seems normal to us is determined by what we have been taught. There are corrections of belief, such as learning that not all "demonstrations" are violent. Important questions get raised, such as whether great leadership is necessary for nonviolence to be effective.   Finally, there are fascinating individual variations in what people notice and emphasize, in how they feel, in the conclusions they draw.

Nonviolence elicits strong feelings and significant, sometimes uncomfortable, thoughts about education and life in general. It is a topic that stirs almost everyone to some degree, upon even brief exposure. Furthermore, most people find that they want to identify with the goals of nonviolence and to express their admiration for its struggles and accomplishments. It is remarkable that a subject not widely known or understood can so quickly command sympathetic understanding, expressed in so many different ways.

Notes

1. Our textbook in this course was *Psychology in Perspective*, by Tavris & Wade. The five broad perspectives on Psychology presented in this text are: Biological, Learning, Cognitive, Sociocultural, and Psychodynamic.

2. *A Force More Powerful* is a video series consisting of six short documentaries on nonviolence-inspired movements for social change. A book of the same title by Ackerman and Duvall recounts these and more stories of nonviolence from the 20th century.

3. *The Children*, by David Halberstam, tells the story of the Nashville sit-in movement through the lives of eight of the young students who led the movement, one of whom was Bernard LaFayette, Jr. The book goes on to trace the involvement of several of these "children" in subsequent events of the civil rights movement, and continues their stories up to the late 1990's.

4. Stanley Milgram was a psychologist who became famous for an experiment on obedience to authority. In this experiment, human subjects who had been told that they were assisting in research on

learning, were instructed to deliver ostensibly painful shocks to another person (who was actually an actor). Surprisingly, many subjects continued to obey instructions even when the shocks were apparently doing serious injury. The study raised questions of many kinds, but at minimum showed that direct instructions from a person in authority have a powerful influence on behavior.

5. *Tough Guise*, a hard-hitting documentary about violence and male socialization by Jackson Katz, was another video seen by this class during the Spring 2002 semester.

6. Philip Zimbardo, another psychologist, showed that even arbitrarily assigned roles can also strongly shape behavior. In his "prison study", some students played the role of guards and others the role of prisoners in a mock prison. In an account that has become legend in the field of Psychology, the study was terminated early because the "guards" went beyond guarding, and began to exhibit cruel and abusive behavior toward their "prisoners".

CHAPTER 6

What Goes On in a Nonviolence Training?

Charles E. Collyer

"Training" usually means some kind of supervised practice of a skill that one wants to learn, or master to a higher degree of proficiency. We can see athletic, musical, vocational, and military training, among others, as fitting this meaning of the term. Intentionally nonviolent thinking and acting are relatively unfamiliar "skills" to most of us at first, and going through nonviolence training is an excellent way to become more familiar with nonviolence quickly. Short-term nonviolence training has played an important role in preparing demonstrators and other workers in social change movements all over the world for what they would encounter as they set out to improve conditions in their communities. For some, whether they have been active in a social change movement or not, the initial experience of nonviolence training is the beginning of a lifelong educational process leading to higher levels of mastery of this "third way" of thinking about life.

"So, what do you actually do in one of these nonviolence trainings?" We get this question a lot.[1] What follows is not a complete answer, because some of nonviolence training involves experiential and cooperative learning; that is, *being there* in a training session or workshop with other people is much more powerful than reading about it. But there is no real mystery to nonviolence training, and here we will try to give a sense of how a workshop is put together and some of the content conveyed to the participants.

We will describe a workshop in *Kingian Nonviolence*, which is based on the work and writing of Martin Luther King, Jr.

There are several other excellent approaches to nonviolence (for example, those of the American Friends Service Committee and the Fellowship of Reconciliation), and we regard the one described here as belonging to a family of related trainings. Some training approaches are Gandhian, some emphasize a religious tradition, some stress social change, and so on. Therefore, while the many varieties of nonviolence training and education do overlap, they are also complementary to each other. One approach will pay more attention to some aspects of nonviolence than others do, and together the different approaches make up a large mosaic of ideas and areas of application.

The Kingian approach described here was developed primarily by Dr. Bernard LaFayette, Jr., in collaboration with his colleagues David C. Jehnsen and Charles Alphin, Sr. Dr. LaFayette was an active participant in the Civil Rights Movement, and worked closely with Dr. King.[2] In Dr. LaFayette's approach, an intensive two-day training experience is the preferred vehicle for introducing nonviolence while doing justice to King's ideas. Here is a typical sequence of topics for a two-day "core" workshop:

Topics in Kingian Nonviolence Training

- Introductions of Participants
- Finding Positive Common Ground
- Types and Levels of Conflict
- A Hegelian View of Conflict
- Historical Perspective: Four Nonviolent Campaigns
- Principles of Nonviolence
- Aggression and Conciliation
- Steps for Nonviolent Problem-Solving
- Bringing Top-Down and Bottom-Up Planning Together
- Large-Scale Exercise
- Closing

A two-day introduction to nonviolence can have a powerful effect on the participants. However, trainers are often asked to present shorter workshops, and the content would then be abbreviated. However, even in a shortened Kingian training we would include some historical perspective on Martin Luther King's work, the Principles of Nonviolence, and the Steps for Nonviolent Problem-Solving.

Let us go through the full list for the two-day training plan, and consider each component in turn.

INTRODUCTIONS OF PARTICIPANTS

The initial introduction of group members to each other is treated as an integral component of the training. Introductions are done in such a way that individuals begin to learn about each other as people, get on their feet and talk, and get a taste of standing in someone else's shoes. Our usual procedure is to have each group member talk with another person for about five minutes, and share answers to some specific questions such as "Where did you grow up?," "What is one thing that most people would never suspect about you?," and "Where would you go on your ideal vacation?" Then we ask each person to introduce their partner in this conversation to the entire group, with a first-person twist: each individual assumes the name and identity of their partner. So if Sally and Ron had been paired for the initial conversation, Sally would start her introduction by saying "Hi, I'm Ron ...", and then go on to relate what she has just learned about Ron, but in the first person.

This type of introduction is a good ice-breaker both for groups of strangers and for groups of co-workers or others who are already acquainted with each other. Taking time for the conversations makes the process of getting started less rushed and more personal. And assuming the identity of another person gives a preview of "putting yourself in another's shoes,"which is a meaningful skill for practicing nonviolence.

Finding Positive Common Ground

People have many positive qualities. They admire good qualities in others, such as strength, humor, quick-wittedness, compassion, and the ability to overcome adversity. They value their important relationships, recognize the value of learning, and - across many religions and cultures - they understand that a reverence for life, the world, and others is a good thing. We use a group exercise early in the workshop to establish that each person in the group has good values, that others also have good values, and that therefore there is reason to identify with other people and respect them as well as ourselves. There are a number of specific exercises that can help accomplish these goals.

Our "better side" needs to be supported, and one goal of nonviolence training is to provide this kind of support. Now, it is true that people have negative qualities too. Every day we receive many reminders that other people can mislead us or be dangerous to us. Our suspicions of others receive support from news stories about shootings and fights, road rage and domestic violence, corruption and brutality. Sometimes this negative bombardment makes it seem that there are two kinds of people, the good and the bad. But in fact, each of us contains both some of the good and some of the bad. In Martin Luther King's words, every one of us has the potential for both great good and great evil. The Russian novelist Alexander Solzhenitsyn expressed the idea this way:

> "Gradually it was disclosed to me that the line separating good and evil passes not through states, not between classes, nor between political parties either – but right through every human heart – and through all human hearts."   - *The Gulag Archipelago p. 615*[3]

We advise the members of our training group that the good side of an enemy, and therefore a large part of our potential commonality with him or her, is very easy to forget. The person that we dislike today almost certainly admires many of the same qualities that we do, and shares many positive qualities with us. But anger and hatred create a strong tendency to dehumanize our opponents. We forget that they are people like us. We also forget that they, or others like them, will still be there tomorrow, and we will again need to interact with them.

Remembering the humanity of our opponents, especially when we are angry, is a skill. Like other skills, it can be improved through practice. During training, we start the practice in a calm and friendly atmosphere. Before moving on, however, we try to make the point that the times when this skill is most needed are also the times when it will be most difficult to carry out.

TYPES AND LEVELS OF CONFLICT

Conflict is a part of life. Differences of perspective, experience, vested interest, ambition, and preference lead us to disagree with each other and to compete with each other. We even invent conflicts in the form of games, sports, and debates. Conflict can teach, invigorate, and entertain. However, we all know that conflict can also get out of hand. Arguments can escalate into violence. In order to understand the origins of violence, and our options for responding to it, it is helpful to take an analytical look at conflict.

We involve our group in distinguishing four different types of conflict. In pathway conflict, the people have the same goal, but are in conflict over how to achieve it. For example, two friends may want to go to Cleveland, one as quickly as possible on the interstate highway and the other by a more scenic and leisurely route. Their conflict is not over where to go, but how to get there. <u>Mutually exclusive conflict</u> (also called goal conflict) involves people who must function together because of family, work, or other ties, but who disagree about their goals. We ask our group to generate examples of goal conflict in the family, at work, and in the community. <u>Distributive conflict</u> describes a situation in which there are not enough resources, and people are fighting for their share. A family example: two teenagers both want to use the family's one car. <u>Value conflict</u> involves a fundamental disagreement over values, about what is right and wrong. The conflicts over abortion rights and capital punishment are familiar, and religious conflicts provide many examples.

Distinguishing different types of conflict can help us to discern what people still have in common (but are likely to minimize) despite their current conflict over paths, goals, resources, or values. For example, people in a pathway conflict have a common goal. It should be said that the types of conflict are not sharply and objectively different. To some extent viewing a conflict as one type rather than another is a choice. Most conflicts have a value dimension, especially to the participants. The important training outcome at this stage is acquiring the view that conflicts can be analyzed, and that the structure of the conflict may contain helpful clues for a participant in the conflict, or for an interested bystander.

Three levels of conflict are suggested as a way to capture the fact that some conflicts escalate toward violence. First is <u>normal</u> conflict, in which disagreement or competition is handled within accepted rules. A second level called <u>pervasive</u> conflict involves stronger emotion, raised voices, combative or defensive postures, and thoughts and words that dehumanize the opponent, setting them up as a target to be attacked rather than a person deserving respect and consideration. Finally, the <u>overt</u> level of conflict involves actual fighting. Where does violence start? For many people, the third stage of overt conflict would be the very definition of violence.   From a nonviolence point of view, violence emerges at the second level in this sequence (but not at the first level with conflict itself).

Our goal is not to eliminate conflict. Sometimes our goal is actually to create it. As practitioners of nonviolence, we are interested in maintaining constructive effort at the normal level of conflict, preventing escalation to the other levels, and intervening to de-escalate to the normal level when necessary. Each of these aims requires the development of conflict-management skills. In an introductory workshop, we point toward this need for learning skills with one or two role-playing exercises on the types and levels of conflict.

Another dimension of a conflict is my distance from it. I may be right in the middle of it (a participant), nearby watching it unfold (a bystander), or at a more remote location. There are nonviolent skills corresponding to these distances, ranging from responding to an immediate personal threat, to changing the conditions and even the social structures that lead to conflict. In general, a person has more options for responding to conflict as their distance from the conflict increases.

A HEGELIAN VIEW OF CONFLICT

Most of us perceive conflict in terms of two adversaries opposed to each other. We assume that the conflict is a contest between these two sides, and that one side will win and the other lose. Martin Luther King was influenced by the philosopher G.W.F. Hegel to view conflict in another way. Consider this quote from one of Dr. King's sermons:

> "But life at its best is a creative synthesis of opposites in fruitful harmony. The philosopher Hegel said that truth is found neither in the thesis nor the antithesis, but in an emergent synthesis which reconciles the two."
>
> - *Strength to Love*, p. 13[4]

The terms thesis, antithesis, and synthesis are from Hegel's treatment of how conflicts evolve over time. The perspective offered by Hegel is that conflicts have a past and a future; they are part of a larger whole. Today's conflict between two adversaries is like a still picture taken out of a movie. Unlike artificial conflicts such as hockey games, the two sides in a real everyday conflict may both win, or they may both lose. They may not stay the same throughout the conflict, because of changes in their knowledge or interests, or because of the intervention of other people. When a new synthesis, a third position acceptable to both of the original adversaries, is found, both sides win. Dr. King saw opportunity in these possibilities. He suggested that creative, nonviolent leadership could often shape the progress of conflicts toward reconciliation of the original adversaries.

How can we discover a synthesis that can reconcile the conflicting positions of thesis and antithesis? There is no formula that will guarantee a satisfactory result. However, there is an approach that is worth trying, and we introduce it in training as a way of turning the Hegelian view of conflict into a rational procedure. In this approach, we look for "threads of truth", that is, valid points or legitimate needs and interests, in both the thesis and the antithesis. Combining the threads of truth from the two opposed positions can give us a "first draft" of a synthesis. At the very least, this exercise gives a third way to look at the overall problem.

HISTORICAL PERSPECTIVE: FOUR NONVIOLENT CAMPAIGNS

The most active period of the Civil Rights Movement was 1955-1968, the years during which Dr. King led a number of campaigns to end legal segregation of the races in the southern

United States. A nonviolence workshop cannot teach all of this history, but we sketch the stories of four campaigns to show the successful use of nonviolence training in community change. For each campaign, the goal is to review the issue that was addressed, some of the people involved, the methods used, and the result that was achieved. We encourage people to study the history of nonviolence in greater detail, and this often becomes an avocation that former workshop participants pursue with enthusiasm.

MONTGOMERY

In Montgomery, Alabama in 1955, the city bus system was segregated by local law, and was notorious in the city's black community for daily mistreatment and humiliation of non-white riders. On December 1, 1955, Rosa Parks was arrested for refusing to give up her seat on a city bus to a white person. Martin Luther King, Jr., a recently-arrived pastor and head of the Montgomery Improvement Association, led a boycott of the city buses that lasted for 381 days. The boycott was opposed by leaders of the white community, and by white supremacists who bombed Dr. King's home. Dr. King insisted on nonviolence throughout the boycott, and won national attention and support for the cause of desegregation. A Supreme Court decision late in 1956 declared the segregated bus system unconstitutional, ending the boycott.

THE FREEDOM RIDES

The Freedom Rides were undertaken in 1961 to challenge southern states to enforce a 1947 law desegregating interstate bus facilities such as washrooms and waiting rooms in bus stations. James Farmer, head of the Congress of Racial Equality (CORE), decided to draw attention to the still-segregated facilities by having a mixed group of black and white people ride Greyhound and Trailways buses from Washington DC to New Orleans. The Freedom Riders were violently attacked in Alabama at Anniston, again in Birmingham, and again in Montgomery. Trained in nonviolence, they did not retaliate in kind. Attorney General Robert Kennedy instructed the Interstate Commerce Commission to issue a new ruling desegregating the interstate busing facilities.

Birmingham

In 1963, one hundred years after the Emancipation Proclamation ended slavery, Birmingham Alabama was, according to Dr. King, the most segregated city in America. The downtown business district allowed black citizens to spend money, but not to sit at lunch counters or to use the stores' fitting rooms or washrooms. Martin Luther King Jr., Fred Shuttlesworth, and others led a boycott of the downtown businesses seeking to desegregate stores and increase their hiring of black employees. There were marches and demonstrations, resulting in the arrests of many people, including Dr. King. It was during this campaign that he wrote the famous Letter from Birmingham Jail. A march across Kelly Ingram Park was met by police violence in the form of dogs and fire hoses ordered by the commissioner of public safety, Bull Connor. An agreement was eventually negotiated with the city, which served as a preview of the federal Civil Rights Act of 1964.

Selma

The voting rights of black people in the south were severely restricted. The campaign in Selma, Alabama in 1965 was part of a major effort by the Southern Christian Leadership Conference, the Student Nonviolent Coordinating Committee, and other groups, to increase the number of black citizens who were registered to vote. Martin Luther King, John Lewis, Hosea Williams, Ralph Abernathy, and other leaders organized three attempts to march from Selma to Montgomery, the state capitol. On Bloody Sunday, March 7, the marchers were beaten by police and a mounted posse as they crossed the Edmund Pettus Bridge. Television broadcasts showing nonviolent demonstrators being ridden down and beaten shocked millions of people. The final march to Montgomery took place two weeks later with participants from across the nation. The Selma campaign was a major factor in passing the federal Voting Rights Act of 1965, which made barriers to voter registration and voting illegal.

Principles of Nonviolence

The heart of this approach to nonviolence training is contained in the chapter called "Pilgrimage to Nonviolence", in Martin Luther King's first book, *Stride Toward Freedom*.[5] Dr. King pauses in the middle of his book about the Montgomery bus boycott to explain the development of his approach to nonviolence. He reviews his educational history and some of the intellectual influences he carried away from his studies at Morehouse College, Crozer Theological Seminary, and Boston University. (A more detailed account of this history and of the principles of nonviolence is available in the book *Search for the Beloved Community*, by Kenneth Smith and Ira G. Zepp Jr., and in *The Social Vision of Martin Luther King, Jr.*, also by Ira G. Zepp, Jr.[6]) Dr. King positions himself in critical opposition to both capitalism and communism, although he finds valuable ideals in both. He distinguishes nonviolence from pacifism. And then, in the last few pages of the chapter, he presents six principles of nonviolence that, for him, are the guiding principles of the boycott and of his overall mission. In nonviolence training we present these principles, and get our groups to alternately challenge and defend them.

MARTIN LUTHER KING'S SIX PRINCIPLES OF NONVIOLENCE

1. Nonviolence is a way of life for courageous people.

2. The Beloved Community is the framework for the future.

3. Attack forces of evil, not persons doing evil.

4. Accept suffering without retaliation for the sake of the cause.

5. Avoid internal violence of the spirit as well as external physical violence.

6. The universe is on the side of justice.

These principles challenge human beings to take a "high road." While they are obviously nice words, the principles will not be considered for serious adoption by most people until they have spent some training time on both the reasons for adopting such ideals and the practical difficulties of living up to them. Interestingly, most people recognize that they <u>want</u> to accept these principles, but fear that the real world makes it too difficult to do so. Here are some initial reactions to each principle:

SAMPLE OBJECTIONS TO EACH OF KING'S SIX PRINCIPLES

1. Nonviolence means not wanting to fight. Sounds like being a coward to me.

2. Community? Why should I put up with people I don't like?

3. What about evil people? Don't they deserve to be attacked?

4. Isn't it stupid to let yourself – a good person – get hurt?

5. My feelings are what they are, violent or not. It's healthy to let them out.

6. Are you kidding? The world is going to hell in a handbasket.

These objections reveal some strong initial resistance to nonviolence. We often defend ourselves against nonviolence as if it were a threat. One of the reasons Martin Luther King stood out as a great leader is that he challenged this resistance. He suggested that the reasons for nonviolence were so strong that we needed to overcome our fears of it. How would Dr. King answer the objections listed above, and others like them? Here are some suggested directions of response:

1. **Courage.** First, there is the matter of courage. Young boys, full of bravado and physical courage, are often frightened by the prospect of embarrassment and ridicule. Once a mean-spirited bullying mood sets in among their friends, they are compelled by this fear to go along. Peer pressure is just as strong for most adults. The courage referred to in Dr. King's first principle is often the courage to act rightly rather than in conformity with group pressure. On the other hand, the readiness to fight is often not a sign of courage but a giving-in to impulse, panic, and expectation. Nonviolence asks us to measure our responses to others, and not to be deluded about what requires courage.

2. **The Beloved Community.** The phrase "beloved community" needs to be made more concrete and accessible for most participants in a training session. What does it really mean? In "Pilgrimage to Nonviolence," Dr. King proposes that our goal in a conflict should not be to defeat and

humiliate our opponent, but to win his or her friendship and understanding. That is, how we act toward our enemies is the test of whether we are moving toward or away from the beloved community. It is difficult to look beyond the moment and decide to treat our enemy decently, and it is precisely this that nonviolence challenges us to do.

3. **Attacking Evil but not People**. The third principle asks us to keep "personalities" out of our efforts to solve problems. Here we are urged to remember that people are not simply good or bad, but a complex mixture of traits and tendencies. Gilligan's (1996) studies of violent criminals support the idea that even very "bad" men are a tragic mixture of beliefs, defenses, and vulnerabilities which invite sympathy upon close examination.[7] The terrible damage done by some of these inmates is evidence not just of personal depravity but of external conditions that if changed could have averted the damage. We are often diverted from solving problems because we fix our emotional energy on revenge against individuals, and because upon getting our revenge through hurting or incarcerating the guilty, we just stop. Martin Luther King was acutely aware that personal animosities continually threatened both his supporters and those who opposed him. He repeatedly sought a detached and firm but courteous way of prodding both sides to address the issues rather than insulting and spitefully undermining each other.

4. **Suffering**. Dr. King forthrightly confirms what many people experience as a great fear: that a commitment to nonviolence may call for suffering. This suffering may occur when a nonviolent person is attacked by a violent person. More commonly, it may occur whenever a

nonviolent person puts him- or herself in an uncomfortable position for a good cause. It should be emphasized that the fourth principle does not send people out to endure just any kind of suffering. There is already plenty of suffering in the world, some of it accidental but much of it unnecessary. The suffering at issue for Dr. King is the purposeful suffering that may be necessary in order to right a wrong, and which therefore can be redemptive not only for the person who suffers but for others as well.

5. **Internal Violence and Love**. In discussing the fifth principle's admonition to avoid internal violence of the spirit, Martin Luther King wrote at length in "Pilgrimage to Nonviolence" about love. His approach was taken from the content of classic sermons on three Greek terms for love: <u>eros</u> or romantic love; <u>philia</u> or friendship; and, of course, <u>agape</u>, a general, unconditional good will toward others. Asked to say what should replace internal violence such as anger, hatred, profane self-talk, and deprecation of oneself and others, Dr. King would say that agape should be cultivated and practiced as a central part of the nonviolent way of life.

6. **A Just Universe**? For Dr. King, there was a religious underpinning for the belief that the universe is on the side of justice. In asking practitioners of nonviolence to be confident about this principle, he was asking a step that was relatively easy and natural for the faithful but difficult for many of his more secular followers. One of our ways to present this principle in a non-religious way is to approach it through a thought experiment about preferences. Imagine that events in the human universe can be sorted into five boxes: the intentionally good, the

accidentally good, the neutral, the accidentally bad, and the intentionally bad. When asked to change the universe by throwing out one box, almost everyone chooses to discard the box containing intentionally bad events. This strong preference is convincing evidence for most people that the universe's scales are at least tipped toward good values such as justice.

In a training workshop, participants would spend time in small groups generating challenging questions about King's Principles. Then, working on the questions posed by another group, the groups would try to formulate answers to the questions that Dr. King himself might have given. This practice in "thinking like King" avoids pressuring people into a premature uncritical acceptance of nonviolence, and provides insight into nonviolence as a way of thinking that can be learned.

Aggression and Conciliation

The "aggression / conciliation" model is an outgrowth of Dr. King's third principle about not personally attacking human beings whose actions may have been evil. It begins with a conception of a person, "you," facing a "problem". Imagine, as in the accompanying diagram, that "you" have two large repertoires of response, called Aggression and Conciliation. The "problem" also has two parts, called Conditions and Persons. Aggression consists of all the high-energy, attacking, oppositional things you are capable of doing. Conciliation consists of all the accepting, understanding, considerate things you can do. Conditions refer to the parts of the problem that exist apart from any specific individuals who are associated with the problem. Persons refer to the individuals who enforce those conditions at the moment.

The aggression / conciliation model is a guide for how to

direct your responses appropriately with the aim of solving the problem. Two things are recommended: directing Aggression toward Conditions, and directing Conciliation toward Persons:

You:		The Problem
Aggression	➜	Conditions
Conciliation	➜	Persons

The model also recommends that two errors be avoided: directing Aggression toward Persons, which tends to set up a cycle of hostility and violence, and directing Conciliation toward Conditions, which amounts to accepting the problem without trying to solve it. Note that Dr. King's third principle is about directing Aggression toward Conditions, and avoiding Aggression toward Persons. The aggression / conciliation model simply fills out the principle with the other two pieces of advice about conciliation. Groups can be asked to analyze a current community conflict that has become "personal", and make recommendations for how it might be handled differently.

The aggression / conciliation model can be appealing to audiences because of its symmetry and completeness in comparison to other approaches. A young man approached one of us after a workshop and thanked the trainers specifically for teaching him about aggression and conciliation. He explained that the model did more than just repeat the often-heard demand that he not fight with people. The part about directing Aggression toward Conditions "gives me something to do with my anger", he said.

Steps For Nonviolent Problem-Solving

Martin Luther King's famous "Letter from Birmingham Jail" is a classic essay on purposeful action. It was written as a response to members of the white clergy who had urged Dr. King and his colleagues to avoid confrontation, and instead wait for the gradual progress of civil rights in Birmingham. Dr. King replied that the time had come for action, and explained that the actions of the campaign to desegregate Birmingham were not impulsive, but the result of a deliberate planning process. He listed the four steps of this process as "… collection of the facts to determine whether injustices exist; negotiation; self-purification; and direct action."[8] In today's training curriculum, we teach nonviolent problem-solving using a framework of six steps whose roots are in Dr. King's Letter:

Six Steps for Nonviolent Problem-Solving

1. Information Gathering

2. Education

3. Personal Commitment

4. Negotiation

5. Direct Action

6. Reconciliation

These steps are meant to be applicable from the individual and family levels to the community and global levels. They stand in contrast to impulsive, hostile, threat-driven responses to problems. The steps are very consistent with many programs of rational problem-solving found in business, psychology, and philosophy.

The first step, Information Gathering, is presented along with the advice "Doubt your first impression." The fallibility of first impressions based on little information is stressed. The need to actively seek out information from appropriate sources can be illustrated with examples generated by the group: "Have you ever felt foolish because you jumped right into a conflict making a totally wrong assumption about what was going on?" In many training groups someone will correctly observe that a problem might very well be solved at the first step (Information Gathering), by getting good information that had been lacking.

The second step, Education, goes along with the first. Education means providing information to other "stakeholders" in the situation. Often the information may need to be framed in terms of the interests and way of thinking of the stakeholder in question. For example, the motivation for renovating a city's playgrounds may be most effectively strengthened among law enforcement officials and among family service agencies using somewhat different arguments. A training group member might very well point out that solutions can emerge at this step by overcoming earlier miscommunications.

The steps of Information Gathering and Education give nonviolence a strong affinity with the social sciences and point to a need for nonviolent leaders to learn the principles of good research and effective communication.

The third step, Personal Commitment, is a very Kingian step. (We have not found this one in textbooks on the psychology of problem-solving, but perhaps it belongs there.) Dr. King found through experience that difficult problems, once they were well-understood, called for courage and strong personal commitment by the people attempting to solve them. The step he called "self-purification" in the Letter from Birmingham Jail is an acknowledgment that serious reflection and a conscious decision to go forward were necessary for him. Sometimes the decision will be to go ahead, and sometimes to postpone further steps if the problem is not "ripe" to be solved right now. In either case it is important for the decision to be deliberate, and based on a good understanding of the situation.

Negotiation brings people with different positions together

to discuss the problem, offer proposals, and attempt to more fully understand each other's underlying interests. There are many treatments of negotiation as an art and a set of management skills. One popular approach that has a strong nonviolent flavor is described in the book <u>Getting to Yes: Negotiating Agreement Without Giving In</u>, by Roger Fisher, William Ury, and Bruce Patton.[9]   Like Martin Luther King, the authors of this book recommend close attention to one's opponent in a negotiation, seeking to understand the needs and interests that lie behind that person's public position. Also like Dr. King, <u>Getting to Yes</u> stresses the availability of win-win outcomes in most negotiating situations, and emphasizes the desirability of negotiating to a conclusion in which nobody walks away as a loser.

But sometimes negotiations break down. Here is where the fifth step, Direct Action, may come in. The action chosen should be appropriate to the problem at hand. In the Montgomery boycott, people stayed off the city buses, while in the Freedom Rides people rode the interstate buses. In each case, the action was appropriate to the issue, and served to create tension toward changing entrenched segregation. The purpose of Direct Action is to return to the step of Negotiation. In Dr. King's words:

"You may well ask: 'Why direct action? Why sit-ins, marches, and so forth? Isn't negotiation a better path?' You are quite right in calling for negotiation. Indeed, this is the very purpose of direct action. Nonviolent direct action seeks to create such a crisis and foster such a tension that a community which has constantly refused to negotiate is forced to confront the issue."

- Why We Can't Wait,
p. 79 (Letter from Birmingham Jail)

Note that Direct Action is not the centerpiece of nonviolence, although for many people examples such as sit-ins, boycotts, and marches are the first things that the word nonviolence brings to mind. Direct Action is the fifth step, not the first. And it is only undertaken conditionally, if earlier steps have not solved the problem.   Protests and demonstrations are sometimes carried out impulsively and out of strong emotional reactions to being offended or threatened. However, this type of direct action should be distinguished from actions that are in the spirit of nonviolence.

Some people will point to Dr. King's deliberate fostering of tension through direct action as evidence that he himself used pressure tactics to get what he wanted from his opponents. To these critics, creating tension and crisis does not seem to fit with their idea of nonviolence. In response to this position, we note that nonviolence is an active, not a passive, approach. We also note that in a democracy, using negotiation and nonviolent direct action stand in contrast to bullying by autocrats and bigots, which represents another approach to "problem-solving." Nonviolence achieves results through political rather than violent means, but without guaranteeing that the process will be comfortable for everyone involved.

The sixth step, Reconciliation, represents a high standard indeed. To the extent possible, the solution of problems should move us closer to the Beloved Community. Reconciliation means that the original opponents in a conflict, and all the stakeholders, can respect one another, understand each other's perspectives, and work together constructively. A friend of ours who is a nonviolence trainer and a police lieutenant keeps the goal of reconciliation in mind as he deals with perpetrators of crimes and angry victims. He reports that the thought of reconciliation tomorrow has a powerful effect on how he interacts with people today who would otherwise "push his buttons."

In many specific instances, reconciliation may be difficult to achieve in the short term. We may have to settle for a disgruntled compromise, for people "agreeing to disagree," for parties simply separating so that they do not continue to hurt each other, or for arbitration that leaves one side much less satisfied than the other. In many books, these outcomes count as conflict resolution. We prefer to think of them as temporary solutions that may eventually achieve nonviolent reconciliation. A helpful thought here is that problem-solving does not necessarily follow the timetable in my head, or yours.

Bringing Top-Down and Bottom-Up Planning Together

Many attempts to solve community problems fail because there is no knowledgeable and respected person on the scene to whom everyone can talk, and who can talk to them. Authority figures make pronouncements that ring hollow to people living in neighborhoods. Average members of the community, who have important things to say, are disregarded by those who have the power to implement their ideas. The people at the grassroots of the problem come to disrespect and caricature the officials in power, and the officials in turn disrespect and caricature the people they are supposed to serve.

From a nonviolence perspective, the built-in differences between official leaders and average community members create a continuing need for bringing "top" and "bottom" together. Nonviolent leadership can seek to bridge the gap between sides that are far apart. Some of the philosophy and skills of nonviolence introduced earlier in the training can now be applied to this type of situation.

For example, we ask our group to remember that both leaders and ordinary community members are human beings with their own perceptions of the community and its problems.

We remember that people may already be making the mistakes of personalizing the conflict (aggression toward persons) or apathetic withdrawal (conciliation toward conditions). We consider that both sides may have some valid points to make (threads of truth in both thesis and antithesis). We hold to the goal of getting people to work together (seeking not to defeat and humiliate the opponent but to win their friendship and understanding). How can nonviolence guide two sides toward a good outcome?

In general, the nonviolent leader or mediator uses the six steps and the aggression / conciliation approach with each side, repeatedly. With one side, we demonstrate that we understand the problem from their point of view including their needs and aspirations that extend beyond the current problem. We seek to establish common ground from which the two sides can begin to work together on meeting shared needs. We encourage each side to see the other as a potential ally rather than a permanent enemy. We also encourage each side to consider its relationship to such constituencies in the community as women and minority groups, youth and students, progressive and voluntary organizations, businesses, educational institutions, religious and interfaith settings, and government agencies.

This topic in the training has traditionally been called "Top-Down / Bottom-Up". The image is of a nonviolent planner and mediator helping two sides to create a synthesis out of their originally opposed positions. This role may or may not be successful on our own timetable in any specific instance. But it is certain that many community problems have remained unsolved, and many misunderstandings between parts of a community have remained to fester for years, because the community lacked some members who were willing and able to play this role.

LARGE-SCALE EXERCISE

Throughout a two-day training there are many opportunities for short role-playing exercises, in which group members can act out conflicts, or answer a question as if they were Martin Luther King, for example. Toward the end of the second day, we usually engage the group in a larger-scale exercise that can draw on several skills from the training. Here we describe one exercise called Joy City. The emphases in this exercise are to practice Information Gathering and Education in a way that involves as many stakeholders as possible, and to go beyond symptoms to look for root causes.

The scenario: Joy City is a hypothetical community of mixed cultures located about fifty miles from where the group is meeting. There is one high school, grades 9-12, and one junior high school, grades 6-8. In the past few years the calls for police service, drug arrests and homicides among youth have increased. There have been several fights at the high school since school started last month, and last evening a young girl was killed by a stray bullet as she left the high school. Witnesses informed the police that a group of youths had been arguing in front of the school with guns just before the shooting started.

The training group is divided into small groups of 3 or 4 people each. The small groups are given 15 minutes to (1) list information they would need to determine the causes of violence in Joy City; (2) to indicate how they would involve various leadership and stakeholder groups in the community; and (3) to decide how they would spend a one-time grant of $100,000 (or make actual use of some other resource) toward solving the problem faced by the community.

At the end of the small-group work, a trainer would call everyone together for a comparison of ideas. There will be plenty of opinions and desire for discussion at this stage. Ideas will emerge that range widely in approach, emotional tone, and emphasis. Many proposals will reflect the topics introduced during the training. It is unlikely that one approach will emerge that everyone agrees is the perfect solution. Almost everyone will feel that they have learned something valuable from ideas that others in the group have put forward.

By this stage, most people in the group will be able to recognize ideas that illustrate the philosophy and methods of nonviolence. Where these ideas seem inadequate, group members will often point out how a proposal could be strengthened and still be nonviolent. The idea that *there may not be a perfect solution, but there are nonviolent approaches that are preferable to "enemy-thinking"*, can be voiced by a trainer, but the group will probably see this without the trainer's help.

CLOSING

At the end of our time with a training group, we like to form a circle and close the training in a way that allows people to reflect briefly on nonviolence and on their experience together. One way to do this is to ask each person to offer one word that captures their reaction to the training and their feeling about nonviolence. Some of the words that we often hear are *energizing, humbling, inspiring, hopeful, transforming, and worthwhile*.

OUR THOUGHTS ON THE EFFECTS OF TRAINING

Based on many training experiences, we believe that an introduction to nonviolence along the lines we have described in this chapter has several positive effects on most of the members of a training group:

❑ Participants in a nonviolence training are reminded through the values exercise that each person has good values, and that while there are differences between people, there is also positive common ground.

❑   Nonviolence training fills in gaps in peoples' knowledge about Martin Luther King, Jr., about the legacy of the civil rights movement, and about the current concerns and functioning of communities, especially in the United States.

❑   The training encourages people to examine their own beliefs and values, and to consider discrepancies between values and practices. It challenges people to consider their life choices and strategies for meeting their needs.

❑   The affirmation of personal worth and the acceptance of needs, combined with the challenge to change strategies, is an honest approach that can appeal to at-risk youth and others who are cynical about attempts to change them as people. The strength of character and courage required to live nonviolently elevates the approach above the myth that "turning the other cheek" is a punk's way out, that anyone who is nonviolent is simply afraid.

❑   Presented as both philosophy and methodology, nonviolence "rings true" to many people in management and human service roles. It captures the complexity and texture of everyday work with people by emphasizing the practical value of a positive approach, while not shrinking from the difficulties of dealing with the negative side of human nature.

❑   Training also allows individuals to consider embracing a potential lifestyle change along with a group of people who have shared the experience. New behavior can be tried out and supported, and people often develop a sense of mission together. The training is an opportunity for people to make a commitment to a "higher road". Many people are surprised to discover that they seem to have been waiting for this opportunity. We have been told that the training has energized and given new motivation to people; that it has transformed their way of thinking about others; and that it has given group members a new framework or paradigm for thinking about solving problems and managing conflict.

❑ These anecdotes have been confirmed by research. Dr. Maram Hallak developed measures of the degree to which this type of nonviolence training reliably produces positive change in attitudes and knowledge. Changes are evident both immediately following training, and at followup several months later.[10]

CONCLUSION

As this account no doubt reveals, we feel rewarded beyond measure in our roles as nonviolence trainers. Although we have become strong advocates of this type of training, we try as professional educators and researchers to keep things in perspective. Nonviolence training seems to meet a need, but it must be regarded as a work in progress rather than a finished product. It is a type of intervention that demonstrably has a positive effect on peoples' attitudes, knowledge, and skill potential. It also seems adaptable to the needs of many different audiences. As we go forward, we have adopted a "continuous improvement" approach to the further development and evaluation of nonviolence training. We believe that this approach is in keeping with the spirit of nonviolence itself, and with Gandhi's advice to continue experimenting with it.

Notes

1. This chapter was written by CEC, with help from Abu R. Bakr, a nonviolence trainer and Special Assistant to the President of the University of Rhode Island. Abu has also directed the Office of Professional Development, Leadership, and Organization Training at URI.

2. A curriculum source book for this approach is the "Leader's Manual": LaFayette, Jr., B. & Jehnsen, D. C. (1995). *The Leader's Manual: A structured guide and introduction to Kingian nonviolence: The philosophy and methodology*. Galena OH: Institute for Human Rights and Responsibilities.

3. Solzhenitsyn, A. (1992). The Gulag Archipelago: 1918-1956. An Experiment in Literary Investigation. Vol. III. New York: HarperCollins.

4. King, Jr., M. L. (1963b). *Strength to love*. Philadelphia: Fortress.

5. King, Jr., M. L. (1958). *Stride toward freedom: The Montgomery story*. San Francisco: Harper.

6. IGZ's work on King's Pilgrimage can be found in his book with Kenneth Smith, and at greater length in the published version of his doctoral research. The two sources are: Smith, K. L. and Zepp, I. G. (1998). *Search for the beloved community*. Valley Forge PA: Judson; and Zepp, Jr., I. G. (1971). *The Social Vision of Martin Luther King, Jr*. New York: Carlson.

7. Gilligan, J. (1996). *Violence: Reflections on a national epidemic*. New York: Vintage Books.

CHAPTER 7

There's More to Nonviolence Than I Thought

Charles E. Collyer

The nonviolent approach does not immediately change
the heart of the oppressor. It first does something to
the hearts and souls of those committed to it. It gives
them new self-respect; it calls up resources of strength
and courage that they did not know they had. Finally
it reaches the opponent and so stirs his conscience that
reconciliation becomes a reality.

-Dr. Martin Luther King, Jr.[1]

One night in Montgomery, Alabama, Martin Luther King
Jr. stood in front of his home, which had just been bombed.
At the time, he was the leader of the bus boycott, begun on
December 1, 1955 when Rosa Parks refused to give up her
seat on a city bus to a white person. The aim of the boycott
was to end the city's long-standing official policy segregating
whites and blacks on the buses. Facing Dr. King that evening
was a crowd of his supporters, angry that their leader's house
had been attacked, and especially angry that Mrs. King and
the couple's first child had been placed in danger of losing
their lives. Dr. King's friends felt they had more than enough
justification to seek revenge. Some of them had weapons, and
they were ready to retaliate against white citizens and their
property. All it would take was a word from Martin Luther
King.

Dr. King told his friends to go home and put away their
weapons. He reminded them that their boycott had a great
purpose, and that to resort to violence would be to throw all

their work away. He reassured them that he and his family were all right. Somewhat calmed, his followers did as he asked. In her later recollection of that time, Mrs. King identified that night as one of the most important moments of the Civil Rights Movement. The boycott went on to win an important victory in the Supreme Court. Montgomery was the first of Dr. King's major campaigns aimed at ending legalized racial segregation in the southern states, and its success made a profound impression all around the world.

This story illustrates the value of nonviolence as an approach to solving difficult problems. Turning away from violence not only saved lives that night, but preserved the credibility and momentum of a movement for social change; it drew admiration and support for Dr. King and his cause; and it provided an example of people choosing, against the pull of their own impulses, to get beyond their present desire for revenge in order to win a larger prize.

Over the past century, the most famous examples of nonviolence in action have been the two career-long campaigns of Mohandas K. Gandhi in India and of Martin Luther King Jr. in the United States. Nonviolent methods have also been used in opposition to virtually every war, to the nuclear arms race, to military conscription in many countries and to many types of economic exploitation and political repression. The exercise of democratic methods such as voting, and the balance of power among branches of a government can be seen as nonviolent alternatives to violent coercion. So can the rational and humane problem-solving methods of good leaders and managers. Many of the world's religions and cultures have contributed to the literature of nonviolence. And nonviolence has heroes all over the world, from the Buddha to Baha'u'llah (founder of the Baha'i faith) and from Danilo Dolci ("the Gandhi of Sicily") to Aung San Suu Kyi (recipient of the Nobel

Peace Prize for her opposition to the military rulers of Burma). There are many types and flavors of nonviolence all over the world.

The authors of this book favor a broad and inclusive approach to nonviolence. But in this book we can only discuss a few parts of this very large field. We have focused on linking the ideas of King and Gandhi with everyday problems of living -- with solving problems that people face, both as individuals and as members of groups and communities. Our goal is to open up the topic of nonviolence for wider discussion and application by as many people as possible.

It is easy for people to recognize an instance of nonviolence when, as in the story about Dr. King, a person visibly turns away from violence in a situation where we might have expected violence to be used. Nonviolence is also at work in situations that are less dramatic, but that also involve turning away from hostility and "enemy-thinking." Here are some examples:

- ❑ In a dispute between family members, nonviolence could mean finding a time to discuss the issue when the anger has subsided.

- ❑ In physically threatening situations, nonviolence could mean trying to talk first rather than automatically fighting or giving in.

- ❑ In a business negotiation, nonviolence could mean trying to satisfy the other side's needs as well as your own.

- ❑ In parenting, nonviolence could mean showing children how to solve problems in a step-by-step way, teaching respect for others, or modeling the values of patience, humor, and responsibility.

❑ In political action, nonviolence could mean taking the time to understand the positions, motives, interests, needs, capabilities, and limitations of all the parties involved.

❑ In dealing with highly volatile community conflicts, nonviolence could mean seeking "win-win" solutions in which everyone's needs and interests are identified and respected.

In all of these situations, nonviolence means working with others respectfully and in a spirit of sensible problem solving. The examples above are stated in positive rather than negative terms, and they use the word "could" to emphasize that we usually have more than one nonviolent option to choose from. In each example, nonviolence would also include avoiding insults and attempts to degrade or humiliate others, as well as refraining from physical violence.

Nonviolence is a large topic. It is a rich and rewarding subject for study, practice, reflection, and sharing with others. And nonviolence is not one "pure" idea. People with diverse points of view can understand it differently. Some people are nonviolent for practical reasons, because they can only get what they want using nonviolent methods. Other people try to live their whole lives nonviolently, because they believe in nonviolence as a basic principle. There are also people who are somewhere in between. Our view in this book is that nonviolence is not one rigid set of rules, but a family of approaches that have some ideas in common.

ASPECTS OF NONVIOLENCE
We propose to break nonviolence into five parts or aspects: opposition to violence, caring about others, goal-orientation, facing reality, and personal investment. Why are we taking

this approach, and why these five aspects?

The authors of this book have introduced nonviolence to many people: students (from elementary school to graduate school), adults in community workshops and churches, and special groups such as prison guards, mental health workers, and teachers. Over and over, people have returned from their first few hours of exploration in nonviolence with such reactions as these:

❑   "There is more to nonviolence than I thought."

❑   "I thought it was just about 'turning the other cheek', but nonviolence is so much more."

❑   "I had no idea of all the other implications."

We believe that the five aspects of nonviolence discussed in this chapter begin to capture what people mean when they express the feeling that there is "more to nonviolence" than they had expected. And we would predict that anyone studying the traditions of nonviolence would soon find that these five concepts are closely intertwined. In keeping with our broad-based approach, we use the term "nonviolence" to tie all of them together.

I. Opposition to Violence

Ahimsa, noninjury, is one of our two "origins" of nonviolence, and is of course at the very core of what people learn from exposure to nonviolence in training, in courses, or through reading.

Being opposed to violence is implied by the very word "nonviolence." But students will find that opposition to violence itself breaks down into more than one idea. There are three ideas in particular that deserve to be highlighted: (i) not committing violence ourselves (this comes closest to the root idea of *ahimsa*); (ii) not cooperating with violence committed by others (a twist on *ahimsa* developed by Thoreau, Tolstoy, Gandhi, and others); and (iii) finding alternative, creative ways to respond (often the most surprising and rewarding part of opposing violence, and the part emphasized by the social sciences and applied fields such as counseling).

Not Committing Violence Ourselves

Wouldn't it be great if our wish, "Let others be nonviolent," could make this a nonviolent world? Why doesn't it work that way?

Each of us sees our own violence as justified. We say things like "She hit me first", "He had it coming", or "I had to teach him a lesson." These statements are rationalizations for a choice we made to be violent.

Usually when a person commits an act of violence, he or she justifies it in terms of self-protection or self-defense. I might be striking back at you to retaliate because you punched me in the nose. Or I might be part of an army invading your country as a precaution before you can invade my country. Whether it is retaliatory or precautionary, I probably tell myself that the violence is necessary in order to protect myself from you harming me.

When harm is extended to include disrespect, I can construct a justification for resentment, hostility, and even physical violence in response to almost anything that makes me feel even slightly misused. Disrespect opens the door to violence, by making my retaliation feel proper, and even necessary.

Nonviolence asks us to question this way of justifying violence to ourselves. On the one hand, we consciously deplore violence and want to get rid of it. But, almost instinctively, we reserve the right to be violent in our own defense. Now, if all violence is to be justified in terms of self-defense, we have not moved anywhere. To break out of this pattern of thinking, we need to take responsibility for ending our own violence, acting so as to discourage violence by others if possible, and looking for ways and means other than violence to protect and defend ourselves.

Making the decision not to commit violence ourselves is very scary for most people. It feels like exposing ourselves to danger. Actually, this decision makes little or no difference in the external dangers that we usually face. However, deciding not to commit violence reduces the danger that we pose to others, and – because people tend to reap what they sow - the likelihood that our behavior will provoke others to violence. Considering all the everyday forms of violence in which we might participate (just think of road rage as one example), the decision not to commit violence ourselves can be an important step toward making our own world safer.

Not Cooperating With Violence Committed by Others

The large-scale violence of British colonial rule in India was the target of several noncooperation campaigns led by Gandhi. For example, in the "Salt Satyagraha", Indians defied the British salt monopoly by refusing to buy British salt and instead making their own. Similarly, Martin Luther King led campaigns of economic noncooperation against the abusive Jim Crow system of segregated public buses, restrooms, stores, and other public facilities in the southern United States. When these campaigns were "illegal" under the prevailing laws, they were by definition examples of civil disobedience.

Noncooperation with violence is not limited to civil disobedience. One achievement of the Women's Movement over the past generation has been the creation of agencies and shelters where victims of domestic abuse can find safety and assistance. The shelters and the movement that created them can be seen as a form of active noncooperation with domestic violence.

The literature on noncooperation with governmental authority includes Henry David Thoreau's famous essay "Civil Disobedience" and the Russian novelist Leo Tolstoy's writings in opposition to militarism and the church's support of conscription under the Czars. The stance of conscientious objection to military service is an important and controversial type of noncooperation, but its more recent stories are little known publicly.

Garden-variety bullying is close to home for most of us. Bullies get away with violence when we cooperate with them by being passive bystanders. Obviously one active approach would be to fight with the bully, a response of punitive violence. But a student named Emily in one of our workshops envisioned another active approach. Emily believed that if a large percentage of the people in her high school knew about nonviolence, the peer pressure among students would then operate very differently. For example, if a bullying incident occurred in the hallway between classes, a crowd of students might converge immediately, telling the bully that violence is stupid and that the way to earn respect is to show respect. This would be active noncooperation with a common form of violence. Schools should ask not just how bullies should be punished, but *how Emily's crowd of nonviolent students could become natural to the school's culture.*

Emily's insight was that, although there are many inspiring stories about individuals responding nonviolently in potentially violent situations, we should not ask nonviolence to perform miracles in the midst of a culture that is accustomed to passively cooperating with violence. Rather, we should use nonviolence education to change the culture so that it no longer provides nourishment to violence. For her, nonviolence training was a step in that direction.

Finding Alternative, Creative Ways to Respond to Difficult Situations

Nonviolence does not simply take away the option of violence, to which many people cling as their most obvious means of self-defense. Rather, nonviolence seeks to provide better options for achieving happiness and security. One of the pleasures of learning about nonviolence is in discovering that there is more – much more -- to nonviolence than "not using violence". There are hundreds of stories about nonviolence that are marked by moments of surprise, relief, humor, and unexpected discovery as creative solutions are found to problems that had seemed doomed to violence. Consider this story from the Civil Rights Movement in David Halberstam's book *The Children*[2]:

The Nashville sit-in campaign of 1960, led by a group of Black college students that included Bernard LaFayette, was the beginning of desegregation in that city. The nonviolence-trained students were frequently harassed by groups of young white men who resented the changes that were taking place.

One day, a group of students were walking to a lunch counter demonstration, when a gang of whites attacked them. A student named Solomon Gort was knocked down, and they were beating him. Bernard LaFayette moved to protect Gort by covering him with his own body, whereupon the attackers turned their kicks and blows on Bernard.

The person who had been teaching nonviolent strategy to the students was Jim Lawson, a pastor who had come to Nashville at the urging of Martin Luther King precisely because Lawson had spent time in India studying Gandhi's legacy. Lawson calmly walked up to the beating of Gort and LaFayette, and the gang turned its attention to this new person. Lawson, cool and mature, wasn't fighting, but he was clearly interfering with their business.

The leader of the gang spat on Lawson. Lawson remained calm, and asked the leader for a handkerchief. A handkerchief was given, and Lawson wiped the spit off. Then, noting that the leader wore a leather jacket, Lawson asked him if he owned a motorcycle. He did. Some questions and answers about motorcycles followed, while in the background Gort and LaFayette got to their feet and the students resumed their walk. Rejoining the students, Lawson waved at the gang leader, who just remained still.

Our colleague Bernard LaFayette, the author of this book's Foreword, lived this story, and went on to become a nonviolence educator in the tradition of Dr. King. We will always be deeply moved by Jim Lawson's courage and creativity in the "motorcycle story." To us, this story is a good example of how nonviolence includes much more than just refraining from violence, and how it can involve surprise – a departure from the violent script that people might be expecting events to follow.

A key idea in the practice of nonviolence is that every situation offers us a range of ways in which to respond. Some of these options are more in the spirit of nonviolence than others, and we can decide that we will choose our response from the "more nonviolent" end of the spectrum. We may have difficulty seeing the range of options arrayed before us, perhaps because we have formed strong habits to respond in only one standard way. However, we can learn to see a wider range of options through study, discussion, openness to ideas that are not "obvious", and practice. For many people, it is a big step forward just to begin thinking about the existence of this range of options.

In the motorcycle story, it is important that Jim Lawson's way of transforming the danger of violence into something else involved focusing on *a human connection between adversaries*. Many stories of nonviolence have this characteristic, and we can use it to guide our search for options. Finding alternatives to violence does not have to depend on a random generation of logical possibilities; rather, we can be pretty certain that the alternatives most likely to transform conflict peacefully are those that focus on human relationships.

2. Caring About Others

Increased caring about others is an outcome of nonviolence education that relates directly to the "origin" concept of *agape*. Let's examine some of the ways in which caring manifests itself, and some of the specific obstacles to be overcome.

Charles Collyer and Abu Bakr have an informal scale they use to rate the atmosphere of schools that they visit. At the bottom of the scale are schools where, from the teachers and administrators, one hears things like "These damn kids. They won't listen to a word you say. You can't turn your back on them. You'd better watch out." At the other extreme are schools where one hears things like "These are our kids. It's difficult for them these days. But they are good people. Listen to what they have to say." What do you suppose it is like to be a student in schools at the top and at the bottom of our scale?

We can also imagine a scale for more general use that gives a rough measure of how much people care for other people. At the bottom would be sentiments like "Don't be a sucker. You can't trust anybody. People are no damn good." At the top would be "Human beings are endlessly interesting and wonderful. We have our problems, but just look at what we can do, especially when we work together."

A friend of ours, the blues musician James "Sparky" Rucker,

points out that people have two eyes at the front of their head, rather than one in front and one in back, or one on each side. This means, according to Sparky, that "we can't watch our own backs, so we were meant to look out for each other". Sparky can be a little gruff sometimes, but this idea puts him at the top of our caring scale.

Some people really enjoy and like other people, and others do not. It is easier to teach the knowledge and skills of nonviolence to people who have a positive attitude toward other people and believe in their potential to be friends and allies. Such people start their own pilgrimage to nonviolence with a head start, because they already possess something that the best teachers of nonviolence always try to encourage.

Both Gandhi and King repeatedly spoke of human beings in a way that emphasized their positive potential. For example,

From Gandhi:

> It is the law of love that rules mankind. Had violence [or hate] ruled us, we should have become extinct long ago. And yet the tragedy of it is that the so-called civilized men and nations conduct themselves as if the basis of society was violence.[3]

From King:

> …man is neither innately good nor is he innately bad; he has potentialities for both.[4]

Notice that Gandhi and King are not saying that all people are good, period. They are saying that people are capable of both good and bad, and can *choose* love, justice, nonviolence, and goodness over their opposites.

Can learning about nonviolence improve my attitude toward other people? Evaluations of nonviolence training suggest that the answer is yes. More research needs to be done on this, but the process seems to work as follows:

Nonviolence seeks to find and support what is good in me. That can make me feel good about myself, and give my self-respect a boost. Nonviolence also points out what is good in you. It can remind me that you deserve my respect too. It can motivate both of us to get to know each other, join forces to get bigger jobs done, find our common problems and work on them together, and help each other when one of us is down. In short, maybe our common good qualities should lead us to care about each other.

What prevents many of us from caring for others? There are several forces that can work either for or against caring, including: cultural messages; how we build our identity; how we process our experiences with others; and our world-view or religion.

Cultural Messages

Many cultural messages support the opposite of caring. For example, our culture, for the most part, tells us to care for good people, but to punish bad people. So before we care about other human beings, we are expected to decide which ones are good and which are bad. Many TV shows, movies, and video games encourage this perception of people as either good or bad. In a typical action movie, the villain is painted as unforgivably bad, and the audience builds up hate and fear toward (usually) him. Then toward the end of the movie, when an avenging good guy is finally unleashed to make the bad guy suffer, the audience experiences this revenge as "justice".

"Well", you might say, "some people commit bad deeds. Isn't it naïve to care about them? Won't that just reward and support more bad deeds?" Let us be clear that people who commit bad deeds must be held accountable for them.

Nonviolence and responsibility are emphatically "joined at the hip." But nonviolence requires that we distinguish between holding others accountable for their behavior and acting out our own feelings toward them. A caring and responsible attitude toward wrongdoers would make punishments fit the crime, avoiding personal injury and humiliation, and providing for as much restoration of damage and rehabilitation as possible. The goal should be to find and develop the best potential for good, not to satisfy our temporary craving for revenge. In a great deal of media entertainment however, revenge is equated with justice, and the idea of turning offenders into productive members of the community is barely considered.

It is one thing to be realistically prepared for self-serving and manipulative actions by others. People are not perfect, and we owe it to ourselves to avoid being abused. However, it is easy to go further and, forgetting all the good that can also be drawn out of people, conclude that suspicion should dominate our attitude toward others. A general good will toward others can coexist with reasonable precautions against abuse. We should consider how cultural messages can be created that would encourage this balance.

How We Build Our Identity

A colleague of ours, a college professor, had a disturbing experience. He had just finished a section of his course on the topic of tensions between different ethnic groups in American society, and had asked his students to write brief comments in reaction to this topic. One student wrote that she felt it was necessary for her to hate some other ethnic groups in order for her to "know myself as a member of my own group". This story suggests that identity, the sense of who we are, is defined not only in terms of positive characteristics that belong to us, but in terms of negative characteristics that are ascribed to others.

Why would a person feel less well known to herself without someone to hate? The answer may lie in a commonplace but very powerful bit of human nature.

The people, places, and things that are familiar to us come to seem normal and natural. The unfamiliar then can seem abnormal or unnatural. When we have experienced people – their speech, their customs, their most noticeable departures from the norm – as "abnormal", it is just a small step to becoming prejudiced against them. In this almost automatic way, we can develop a collection of contrasting beliefs about Them (the strange, abnormal ones) and Us (the familiar, normal ones) that become part of our identity, our conception of who we are. We are clean; they are dirty. We are intelligent; they are stupid. We know how to behave; they don't. And so on. These thoughts about Them become excuses not to care about Them as fellow human beings.

Is there another way to build our identity, other than through negative contrasts with others? Certainly. First, we can be aware of how the experience-familiarity-normality chain works to create our prejudices. The beliefs we arrive at are not objective facts about Them, but products of this chain and related thought processes. Second, we can counteract these beliefs through better educating ourselves about the world outside our familiar sphere. For example, education can have an impact by revealing that within any group of Them, there is tremendous variation among individuals. To someone who is familiar with an ethnic or racial group, blanket statements about the group seem to be absurd nonsense. Third, we can use these tools – awareness of our own thought processes and meaningful education – to build our own identity on a solid foundation of knowledge about our own strengths and weaknesses, without lazily leaning on shallow comparisons with other groups.

How We Process Our Experiences With Others

We all have bad experiences with people. We all have good experiences, too. But memory and attention are selective. It is very easy to select our bad experiences to think about and ignore the good ones. If we do this, we can shape our own attitude and mood to be persistently negative. This can set "self-fulfilling prophecies" into motion, in which the reactions we create through our bad attitude come back around to us in the form of hostility and avoidance from other people. And what stronger confirmation of our misanthropic (people-hating) views could we get than the nasty hostility of our neighbors?

Selectivity and self-fulfilling prophecies work the other way too. If we select our best experiences with people to think about, it influences our mood, speech, and actions in a positive way. And what goes around comes around. Projecting a positive attitude usually influences the people around us to return the favor. It is then pretty easy to care about the welfare of those people, because they are being so good to you!

A balanced view of life recognizes that both good and bad things happen to us. It also recognizes that our own actions can become good or bad events in the lives of others as well as our own. (How often have I, through carelessness or otherwise, been a part of what someone else experiences as "Murphy's Law" – that what can go wrong, will go wrong?) There is much more to be said about all this. For the present, however, it is sufficient to note that our willingness to care for others is related to what we select and emphasize in processing our experiences with others.

World-View or Religion

Liberating as it is to "let it go" and turn a problem over to a "higher power", this shift to the supernatural can also relieve us of our responsibility to others, and diminish caring about what happens in this world. The Serenity Prayer, attributed to Reinhold Neibuhr and widely used in Alcoholics Anonymous and similar programs, expresses our need for a balance between accepting and acting: "Grant me the serenity to accept the things I cannot change, the courage to change the things I can, and the wisdom to know the difference." Too much emphasis on the first part can hold us back from caring. Too much emphasis on the second can make us a loose cannon. It really does take wisdom to know the difference.

Both Gandhi and King were religious men, but in a worldly way that made them different from some of the other leaders of their religions. Gandhi directed his Hindu followers away from supernatural fatalism. He emphasized what people could do in this life to free themselves and improve conditions for women and the "untouchables". King criticized other Christian ministers who emphasized getting to heaven upon death over improving social conditions for the living.

3. Goal-Orientation

We can analyze Goal-Orientation into at least two important ideas. One is the concept behind the phrase "Eyes on the Prize"; the other is the requirement that, in solving problems, our methods should be consistent with our goals.

Eyes on the Prize

The wonderful phrase "Eyes on the Prize" is the title of a video history of the Civil Rights Movement, produced by the Public Broadcasting System. The phrase comes from the determined refrain of the freedom song "Hold On" by Alice Wine. Here is the last verse:

> Got my hand on the freedom plow,
> Wouldn't take nothin' for my journey now.
> Keep your eyes on the prize, hold on.

Hold on, hold on!
Keep your eyes on the prize, hold on![5]

Keeping our eyes on the prize means staying focused on our main goal. That is what Martin Luther King was doing when he asked his angry friends to go home. It is a skill that can be learned, and stories like the one about Dr. King are one way to learn. In nonviolence, the skill of staying focused on what is really important is called upon when we must survive moments of anger which threaten to lead us into insulting, threatening, humiliating, or physically hurting others. These moments usually pass, and are followed by a calmer emotional state in which we are less inclined to hurt our "enemy" and more able to work nonviolently to solve our problem with him or her.

The song "Hold On" was part of the rich musical heritage of the Civil Rights Movement. Its message: to be patient, keep working for good, and keep the goal in mind, was a needed reminder to people who were frustrated by the taunts, cruelty and abuse of powerful opponents every day for years and years.

Actually, both King and Gandhi were often criticized for their patience in the face of this abuse. People are easily tempted into lashing back at those who hurt them. But in the long run, it became clear that the patience of these great leaders was a purposeful, restrained choice about how to respond. Their reputations were built by pressing a long-term struggle against injustice while refusing to be baited into short-term violence.

The old advice about moments of anger, that we should "count to ten" (or a hundred) in order to let anger pass, is good advice. But we should also understand that getting through these moments is not done just to demonstrate that we can do it. Staying under control helps us to achieve our goals. The advice would be more complete if it said "keep your eyes on the prize and count to ten".

Consistency of Methods and Goals

Another theme that runs through Martin Luther King's writings is that our means should be consistent with our ends. More exactly,

> *... the means we use must be as pure as the ends we seek.*[6]

Is Dr. King saying more or less that "the end justifies the means"? This more familiar phrase suggests that after we have chosen a good end (a goal), any means (method) is justified in attaining that goal. But King is definitely not saying that. In King's thinking about nonviolence, we choose both our ends and our means, and we need to justify them both. We need to use nonviolence in making both choices, so that consistency comes from means and ends both satisfying a worthy standard. We can undermine a good goal by using evil methods to attain it. And the goodness of our methods will be undermined if we use them to pursue an evil goal.

4. Facing Reality

What does "facing reality" mean? It could spark either of two attitudes: accepting the real world with resignation ("You might as well face reality ... "); or confronting the world as it really is, in order to solve real problems. Here we are interested in the latter, active sense of the phrase. Let us break this aspect of nonviolence into three components: acquiring accurate knowledge; facing unpleasant as well as pleasant facts; and adopting practical strategies and tactics.

Acquiring Accurate Knowledge

Nonviolence aims to create a better world. You can't improve something unless you have accurate knowledge about its current condition, about reality. In his *Letter from Birmingham Jail*, Martin Luther King said that the first step in any nonviolent campaign was the collection of facts to determine whether injustices exist. In a larger sense, information gathering is the first responsibility of anyone who hopes to solve a problem.

There is a great deal of knowledge that we need, both general background to build our understanding of the world, and specific information about a problem at hand. We need to understand about nonviolence itself: its history, philosophy, and breadth of application. We need to understand human nature as well as we can, and with as much generosity and tolerance as possible. We need to know how the world works economically, politically, and technically; the pitfalls and problems that people can face; and ways of bringing help to bear. And we need to understand artistic expression – how people tell in language and music and visual images about their lives.

These are reasons to commit to a life of continual learning and education, in case anyone was looking for a reason to stay in school, go back to school, study research methods, or start in on the study of a worthwhile subject.

Facing Unpleasant as well as Pleasant Facts

A practitioner of nonviolence should not be naïve. The world includes very harsh and unpleasant realities. The arenas in which nonviolence is most needed are environments in which ugly things happen. Women fear bodily injury and death at the hands of current and former lovers. High school students are victimized by gambling, prostitution, drugs, and physical intimidation. Gangs retaliate against each other in brutal ambushes. Co-workers manipulate and sabotage each other for advantage in the workplace. Salespeople tell outright lies dozens of times each day in order to maintain their incomes and their jobs. Arms dealers sell deadly weapons to both sides in wars around the world. This unfortunate list goes on and on.

There is no quick remedy for most of these problems.

Nonviolence does not assume that we can solve difficult problems quickly. It does offer some insights:

❑ violence tends to occur as part of a cycle of mutual retaliation which we need to understand if we are to change it;

❑ likewise, violence pervades systems in which some people oppress and intimidate others;

❑ the perpetrators of violence are degraded by their own actions, and so suffer losses which we need to appreciate;

❑ common ground, that is, shared interests and needs - easily forgotten in conflict – needs to be rediscovered; and

❑ in most conflicts each side owns part of the truth, so that we need to learn from both, even when the truth is embedded in grave injustice.

Nonviolent leaders are sometimes criticized for their willingness to attribute some truths, some value, to an enemy hated by their followers. But one of the ways in which people avoid reality is by refusing to learn from people who are disliked and despised. We can obviously learn more if we *do not avoid any information* that can help us solve difficult problems.

ADOPTING PRACTICAL STRATEGIES AND TACTICS

Gandhi and King were both skilled politicians. They made shrewd judgments every day about all the practical needs of their movements. They picked their battles carefully. They built support for difficult political tasks by bringing people from different classes and interest groups together. Their work was successful because they faced the facts of each situation and worked with the real interests and limitations of the people who were involved. It could not have been accomplished if these leaders had been naïve or impractical men.

However, in a critique of Gandhi's nonviolence, the theologian Reinhold Niebuhr (whom King especially admired) made a distinction between Gandhi's attempts to deal with others out of a spirit of good will, and his political methods. He described the first as a loving attitude:

> Non-violence, for him, has really become a term by which he expresses the ideal of love, the spirit of moral goodwill. This involves for him freedom from personal resentments and a moral purpose, free of selfish ambition. It is the temper and spirit in which a political policy is conducted … rather than a particular political technique.[7]

Physically nonviolent political action, however, like violent methods, is not neutral but coercive:

> Non-violent coercion and resistance, in short, is a type of coercion which offers the largest opportunities for a harmonious relationship with the moral and rational factors in social life.[8]

Though Martin Luther King seems to have been somewhat taken aback by Niebuhr's characterization of nonviolence as a form of coercion, he was definitely inspired by the conclusion of Niebuhr's argument (written 25 years before the Montgomery boycott) as it related to black people in America:

> This means that non-violence is a particularly strategic instrument for an oppressed group which is hopelessly in the minority and has no possibility of developing sufficient power to set against its oppressors.

The emancipation of the Negro race in America probably waits upon the adequate development of this kind of social and political strategy. It is hopeless for the Negro to expect complete emancipation from the menial social and economic position into which the white man has forced him, merely by trusting in the moral sense of the white race. It is equally hopeless to attempt emancipation through violent rebellion.[9]

Both as a student and throughout his career, King must have read this passage of Niebuhr's again and again.

Was nonviolence used coercively by Gandhi, and later by King? The short answer must be yes. Nonviolence has often been used to pressure political and economic powers to "do the right thing". Consider again this passage from the Letter from Birmingham Jail:

You may well ask: "Why direct action? Why sit-ins, marches, and so forth? Isn't negotiation a better path?" You are quite right in calling for negotiation. Indeed this is the very purpose of direct action. Nonviolent direct action seeks to create such a crisis and foster such a tension that a community which has constantly refused to negotiate is forced to confront the issue. It seeks so to dramatize the issue that it can no longer be ignored. My citing the creation of tension as part of the work of the nonviolent resister may sound rather shocking. But I must confess that I am not afraid of the word "tension". I have earnestly opposed violent tension, but there is a type of constructive, nonviolent tension which is necessary for growth.[10]

Here we see clearly King's view of nonviolence as a strong active force, capable of grappling with difficult real-world problems. This view contrasts sharply with the assumption held by many people that nonviolence is a passive or resigned attitude, averse to tension or confrontation.

The strategies and tactics of nonviolence have, for the most part, been developed by disadvantaged people. Its practitioners were not able to get what they wanted by physical force. So they devised ways for relatively powerless people to exert pressure for change in other ways. The invention of nonviolent political action deserves a place in any list of examples of "progress".

5. Personal Investment
Personal investment means the effort and time and sacrifice that each of us puts in to become more nonviolent. Like nonviolence itself, personal investment takes many forms and is related to many other ideas. Let us approach this aspect of nonviolence by considering first the goals of personal investment and then the methods that move us toward these goals.

Goals
There are two broad goals of personal investment: (1) personal development or empowerment, and (2) becoming a more effective agent of social change. There is actually some conflict between those who advertise personal empowerment as an outcome of nonviolence training and those who see such empowerment as secondary to, and even as a distraction from, the goal of social change. We regard both personal development and social change as worthwhile goals. Each provides a good reason for personal investment, and there is no necessary reason for them to be in conflict with each other. In fact, they can complement each other.

Almost all supporters of nonviolence would agree that individual human beings must be instruments of change. To become more effective instruments, they should make a personal investment of time and energy to learn and practice the skills of nonviolence. The personal investment itself can be rewarding, and so can become one of the attractions of nonviolence. Many good programs for youth begin with the rewarding consequences of personal investment as their "lure", often using the term "empowerment" to emphasize the positive effect of learning nonviolent skills on the individual who learns them.

Paradoxically, it is desirable for a practitioner of nonviolence to be quite capable of violence. To abstain from violence only because one is too weak to use it, is not ideal. Better is to be capable of violence, but choose nonviolent options deliberately and consistently. Therefore, one goal of personal development can be to become strong in the ways usually associated with violence. For this reason, martial arts training, especially in philosophically nonviolent disciplines such as aikido, has been chosen by many individuals as part of their personal investment in nonviolence.

There is room for a great deal of variation in the goals adopted by different individuals. In a living tradition like nonviolence, we think it is quite proper for tastes and preferences to come into play. Also, life is not long enough to become a master of every skill, field of knowledge, art, or discipline. The value placed on personal growth itself, and the process of growing toward our goals, are more important than the particulars.

METHODS

Personal investment should probably take the methodological form of a daily program or regimen, in which each of our goals receives some attention. Some people are naturally inclined to such programs, and are very strict about them. Others are more casual. Again, there is room for variation.

Gandhi is the most famous example of a nonviolent leader trying to practice everything he preached, starting with himself.

In Gandhi's case, personal investment took the form of giving up material possessions, alcohol and meat, sex, and many ordinary sources of comfort. His fasts, originally undertaken to put political pressure on his followers and opponents, were eventually also a form of personal self-purification. He believed that his own life was inevitably going to be viewed as an example to others of nonviolence. Therefore, he wanted to be sure that people could learn about nonviolence by observing him. He also wanted to gain the political advantage of being seen as a poor and humble citizen-leader. However, he had a sense of humor about the symbolic side of his asceticism: in the film <u>Gandhi</u> we hear his acknowledgment that it cost a great deal of his supporters' money to keep him in poverty!

Many people, using Gandhi as their example, recoil from the self-sacrifice that they assume nonviolence requires. But in fact there are no "Nonviolence Police" checking up on our degrees of personal investment to ensure that they are adequate! Supporters of nonviolence cover quite a wide range on the dimension of personal investment, from Gandhi-like self-denial to simple opposition to violence at the tactical level.

Overview of the Aspects

We have examined five aspects of nonviolence – five varieties of "discovery" that we have observed in people who are learning about the details of nonviolence for the first time. One of the aspects of nonviolence – opposition to violence – is couched in negative terms. The other four – caring for others, goal-orientation, facing reality, and personal investment – are couched positively. In the end, the valence, positive or negative, of these aspects when briefly labeled, is their least important feature. It is clear to everyone who does some study that nonviolence is a positive, and powerful, concept.

However, the negative valence of the term nonviolence itself may be responsible for the relatively impoverished understanding that so many people have. The purpose of this discussion has been to stimulate your interest in nonviolence by laying out some of its richness for inspection. The intended take-home message is that nonviolence has multiple though related aspects, and can challenge a person with its complexity, its "scariness", its combination of idealism and practicality, its connection to many different problems and fields, its applicability to difficult problems, and its very colorful literature. We hope you will discover more about nonviolence through further exploration, and then pass on this deeper understanding to others.

Notes:

1. Martin Luther King, Jr. From King, C. S. (ed.) (1996). *The Words of Martin Luther King, Jr.* New York: Newmarket Press, p.79.

2. Halberstam, D. (1998). *The Children*. New York: Fawcett, pp. 137-138.

3. From Arun Gandhi's pamphlet *M.K. Gandhi's Wit and Wisdom, p. 40* (no date), Memphis, TN: Gandhi Institute.

4. From the article "Love, law, and civil disobedience," *New South* vol. 16, Dec 1961; quoted in K. Smith & I. G. Zepp, Jr., *Search for the Beloved Community: The thinking of Martin Luther King Jr.* Valley Forge: Judson (1974).

5. Words from the version included in Blood, P. and Patterson, A. (eds.) (1992). *Rise Up Singing*. Bethlehem PA: Sing Out.

6. From the *Letter from Birmingham Jail*, 1963.

7. From Reinhold Niebuhr, *Moral Man and Immoral Society*, New York: Scribner's, p. 246 (1932).

8. *ibid*, p. 250.

9. *ibid*, p. 252.

10. From the *Letter from Birmingham Jail*, 1963.

CHAPTER 8

A Dialogue on Terrorism and Nonviolence

William A. Holmes and Ira G. Zepp, Jr.[1]

A third author, William A. Holmes, visits the book in this chapter. Bill Holmes is a retired United Methodist minister. For 24 years he was the Senior Minister at Metropolitan Memorial, the National Methodist Church in Washington D.C. Before that, he served campus-related churches in Dallas, Denton and Austin, Texas. He is a graduate of Perkins School of Theology, and did post-graduate work at Union Theological Seminary in New York where he studied with Reinhold Niebuhr and Paul Tillich. He presently serves as the Chairman of the Ethics Advisory Committee at Sibley Memorial Hospital. Bill does not identify himself as an advocate of nonviolence. However, readers will recognize in his thinking many of the aspects of nonviolence that this book has been exploring. Perhaps it would be fair to say that while Bill Holmes may not fit into a stereotypical conception of nonviolence advocacy, his "Nieburian realism" makes it possible for him to offer a critique of some principles of nonviolence, while also affirming Christian imperatives that are meant to encompass all people.

This chapter begins with a position paper, Christians and Terrorism, written by Bill Holmes following the terror attacks of September 11, 2001 in New York and Washington DC. Ira Zepp, a friend of Bill's and one of this book's authors, responded to this paper. An exchange of email letters between Bill and Ira followed, in which they attempted to define their positions with respect to each other more clearly. The resulting dialogue, not originally intended for publication, is a window through which we may see core issues of violence and nonviolence, and

the borderlands between them, being explored with respect
– respect both by Bill and Ira for the issues, and by the two
men for each other.

CHRISTIANS AND TERRORISM: A POSITION PAPER
William A. Holmes
November, 2001

I admire Christian non-pacifists who can express respect for
the pacifist position. Reinhold Niebuhr was such a person. For
all of his rigorous critique of pacifism, Niebuhr was an ardent
advocate of the pacifist contribution. In 1940, he wrote: *We
who allow ourselves to become engaged in war, need the testimony
of the absolutist against us, lest we accept the warfare of the world
as normative, lest we become callous to the horror of war, and lest
we forget the ambiguity of our own actions and motives and the
risk we run of achieving no permanent good from the momentary
anarchy in which we are involved.*[2]

As one who has arrived at the non-pacifist position with
a deep respect for Quakers, the historic peace churches, and
others who conscientiously abstain from military action, I want
to argue in this position paper that the Bush administration,
for all its limitations, has offered an appropriate response to the
terrorists' acts of September 11. I intend to state this point of
view as explicitly as I can because, with only a few exceptions,
most of the post-September 11 statements of religious leaders
and church bodies have avoided speaking directly to the use
of military force - whether to its inappropriateness or to its
justification. Such statements have rightfully condemned
the terrorists' attacks as crimes against humanity. They have
appropriately warned against an anti-Arab and anti-Islamic
community backlash. They have properly called for prayer,

Bible study, trust in God, and various non-violent strategies that make for peace and justice. But seldom have such statements taken a position, one way or the other, as to how Christians ought to view and react to the United States resort to force. I think such a clarification is badly needed at this time, and has historic precedent.

The "just war" tradition can be traced to Augustine, who grappled in the fourth century with the undeniable fact that Christian teaching challenges any resort to violence. Augustine opposed wars of aggression and aggrandizement, but he further believed that there were times when the resort to force may be tragically necessary - never a normative good, but a tragic necessity. Through the centuries, there has emerged the concept of the "just war" as the lesser of two evils, and always defined by principles of last resort, proportionality, prudent expectation, and the immunity of noncombatants from direct attack. This has meant that on occasions, Christians like Dietrich Bonhoeffer, with strong presumptions for peace and non-violence, have decided to "sin bravely" for the greater good.

One of the few post-September 11 statements from religious leaders which spoke clearly to the U.S. use of force was from 260 Roman Catholic Bishops in this country. The document, entitled, "A Pastoral Message: Living with Faith and Hope", stated, "No grievance, no matter what the claim, can legitimate what happened on September 11."[3] The Bishops spoke unequivocally, saying the United States "has a moral right and a grave obligation to defend the common good against mass terrorism." And then, for Catholics in uniform, there was the assurance that for them "to risk their own lives in this defense is a great service to our nation and an act of Christian virtue."

The statement is equally forthright in its call for additional humanitarian imperatives. It urges the United States to pay greater attention to "those conditions of poverty and injustice which are exploited by terrorism," and to be more generous in fighting poverty around the world. It includes an appeal for aid to avert the starvation of Afghan civilians this winter and a condemnation of the "unconscionable policies which have led to the deaths from disease and malnutrition, of hundreds of thousands of children in Iraq." The document cautions a need to guard civil liberties at home, and urges a prompt settlement to the Israeli-Palestinian conflict. It concludes affirming "principled nonviolence…is a valid Christian response" and "military force, even when justified and carefully executed, must always be undertaken with a sense of deep regret."

Another example of public support is from a recent speech by Nelson Mandela, who, though not a religious leader, per se, is certainly prominent for his commitment to peace and justice. Speaking to a crowd of more than 10,000 at the University of Maryland on November 14, the 83-year-old Nobel Peace Prizewinner called for a global and unified effort to wipe out "this scourge" of terrorism. While affirming the military initiative of the Bush administration during a meeting with the President two days earlier, Mandela used his speech at the University's fourth annual Sadat Lecture for Peace to reiterate that support. At the same time, he urged a greater fairness in U.S. policy toward Israel and Palestine, and reminded his audience that the divide between the rich and the poor continues to grow and is becoming "a fertile breeding ground for discontent and for extremism and terrorism." He also warned the West against assuming that its brand of democracy is the only answer to the problems of other countries, pointing out that there are nations with governments different from ours that offer greater service and support in meeting the basic needs of their citizens. Mandela, like the Catholic Bishops, found "just cause" for the U.S. resort to force, while placing that force in a context of greater efforts on behalf of poverty and injustice.

It is not my intention to suggest some superior righteousness in the non-pacifist position. On the contrary, that position is compromised by ambiguities, complexities and contradictions. But so is the pacifist position - especially when its commitment to non-violence gives "safe passage" to the malice and aggression of others.

For Reinhold Niebuhr, even during the time he was national chairman of the Fellowship of Reconciliation, his pacifist sympathies were practical and pragmatic. He knew pacifism could only achieve its goal when those who are resisting have a potential ally in the consciences of their opponents, as with the case of Gandhi's struggle against the British. Furthermore, he was always clear about his own complicity in sin, and that his choice of the pacifist philosophy was the lesser of two evils.

By 1932, Niebuhr had left his pacifist position, becoming more and more alarmed by the relentless aggression of Adolf Hitler and the futility of European appeasement. Just before World War II, he was instrumental in founding the periodical, "Christianity and Crisis", in order to counteract a pacifist trend in the Church. War, he believed, horrible as it may be, is preferable to surrender to a totalitarian system.

Niebuhr considered absolute pacifism to be a "very sentimentalized" form of the Christian faith, as well as a dangerous intervention in pragmatic politics. He argued that the Reformation doctrine of justification by faith does not offer a grace that lifts human beings "out of the sinful contradictions of history" and establishes them "above the sins of the world." On the contrary, it is by that grace that we are empowered to confess our sins and be forgiven, knowing that there is no way to live in history without sinning. This assumption does not excuse us from making our best effort to be ethical and moral, but it does deliver us from any pretension or illusion that we are entitled to claims of a superior righteousness. Niebuhr was as hard on non-pacifists as he was on pacifists.

My own choice of non-pacifism in the war against terrorism is a pragmatic choice, predicated on the belief that Osama bin Laden and the al Qaeda network would not likely desist in their jihad against the United States, even if our response to September 11 was a non-violent, non-military response. Such a conclusion finds me inextricably involved in sinful compromises, but no more so - in fact, I think even less - than were I to choose the pacifist position.

The decision to support the use of force against terrorism is certainly no carte blanche endorsement of George W. Bush and all his policies. I voted against him in the election, and I continue to question the U.S. Supreme Court's unprecedented intervention in the Florida electoral process by which he became President. I blanche every time he replicates the absolutist, holy war rhetoric of the other side, referring to the enemy as "evil," and invoking the divine stamp of exclusive approval with "God bless America." I lament his superficial understanding of what it means for America to return to normal when he counsels us to "Get down to Disney World in Florida." Yet, for all my misgiving about the election, the President's use of jihad language, and the commercialization of a horrible tragedy, I am convinced that the United States has no choice but to treat the murders of thousands of civilians as an act of war. President Bush, for all his limitations, has risen to the occasion, and led the nation in a response that Christians can support as a "just war."

Furthermore, to be supportive of our nation's use of force in this instance, need not imply an indifference to our flawed policies and myopic lifestyles. By now, it must be clear to the international community how quick we are to build alliances when a military action is looming, and how reluctant we are to participate in Kyoto and ABM treaties, or to join with other nations in such efforts as banning land mines. It is as though we only round up the posse when the bad guys threaten us. Our policies toward Israel and the Palestinians have not been even handed, and have too often tilted toward a Zionist bias - causing great suffering and privation. Our lifestyle patterns of conspicuous consumption and our inordinate hogging of the world's resources continue to have devastating repercussions for that one out of every three people on this planet who do not have enough food, and the one billion who are literally starving. But the sum total of these, and other U.S. caused injustices, does not add up to a compelling justification for the September attacks against this nation. They may help explain anti-American feelings, and they certainly should be the occasion for national introspection, but it is simplistic and naïve to argue that on September 11 the American people "got what we deserve."

In fact, there is a psychopathology at the root of the terrorists' rage and suicidal actions. The name of that root is modernity, which is both liberating and destabilizing. Paul Hollander, professor emeritus of sociology at the University of Massachusetts - Amherst, writes: *The problems modernity creates are not primarily those of poverty (which it more often alleviates than aggravates) but loss of meaning, the erosion of a coherent worldview and the anxieties created by personal freedom. Traditional societies, though poor, used to be capable of providing their members with a stable, religiously grounded worldview. Modernity undermines this worldview, and the sense of certainty and community associated with it. The cultural relativism and moral uncertainty that modernity unwittingly stimulates lie at the heart of the protest against globalization, the West and the United States. In the Arab world, Israel is hated as much for being an outpost of modernity and Western values as it is for occupying lands claimed by Palestinians.*[4]

Failing to understand the psychopathology behind terrorism is failing to understand the tremendous certainty and security provided by the Taliban's fundamentalist interpretation of Islam and the traumatic sense of loss when old absolutes and certainties are threatened. It is a condition similar to the experience of the white racist who finds cultural identity and financial advantage in segregation, and who is therefore threatened by integration. Or the homophobic person whose sexual identity is secured in the belief that only heterosexuality is normal and God given, and who is therefore threatened by the claim that other kinds of sexual preference could also be experienced as "given", and not necessarily as chosen. Or the macho male who is convinced that masculinity is superior to femininity, and who is threatened by women's rights, women in the work place, and women's shelters. It also occurs to me that sometimes persons who are most clear about the psycho-pathologies behind these aberrations, and who are vigorous advocates for racial minorities, gays and lesbians, and battered women, are unwilling to allow for a psycho-pathology behind acts of terrorism. Instead, they are quick to blame the United States for being the primary cause of its own misfortune.

I conclude as I began, with a sense of genuine indebtedness to those who hold the pacifist position. The white light of their absolutes shines inexorably on the gray ambiguities and inconsistencies of my non-pacifist perspective. And, although I believe their absolutism places them beyond the historical crucible where we are meant to live, they continue to remind me of the truth of Niebuhr's paradox: human sin is "inevitable but not necessary." Or, to say it one more time: The hope for all of us, pacifist and non-pacifists alike, is in the grace of God.

From Ira Zepp, December 4, 2001

Dear Bill,

As usual, your arguments are lucid and irenic, thoughtful and honest, balanced and fair. I love you for it and respect your position. Thank you for the chance to read the paper and, particularly, the questions it raises in my mind. This is my test of good position paper.

1. I am very conflicted, more than you may know, over my position as a non-ideological, but relatively committed pacifist (on a scale of 1-10, I'd be something in the area of 9+). The space between 9 and 10 is the non-dogmatic "Bonhoeffer" part. It is pretty difficult to be "absolute" when you live in contingent, relative history. Just war was formulated when sword and bow were weapons and battlefield lines were carefully drawn. But to the extent just war theory was ever practiced, I don't see how it can be practiced in a nuclear age, much less in an age of sophisticated terrorist wars. One thing Niebuhr taught us was that in our sinful state our capacity for self-deceit is infinite and our talent to legitimize "war" seems to know no bounds. Cf. Afghanistan. Have we duly, with proper delegated authoritative powers, declared war? Is it our last resort? Is our bombing proportionate? When, how, who decides this? What about non-combatants? Do we project a reasonable end to this "war?" As a Christian, I have a tough time giving a positive adjective to war. Would a "more or less, semi-sinful war" be better, more accurate (cf. Niebuhr's "sinful contradiction of history")? Would "unjust war" be more descriptive and honest? Would "nevertheless, in spite of every effort we've made war"

work? Would "war with deep regret" (re: the Catholic Bishops' statement) sound better to God's ears? How about "unsentimental, regretful, realistic war?" How does this language sound before God; can we ask this eschatalogical question?

2. I agree with much that the Catholic Bishops, Mandela, and you say. But why do I feel uncomfortable with it? I'm sure you feel uncomfortable also. On the one hand the Bishops and Mandela say we have a "moral right and grave obligation to defend the common good against mass terrorism" because of a "legitimate grievance" on 9/11. (I agree and Osama bin Laden must be brought to justice. HOW he is brought to justice, or otherwise disposed of however, will be more important than THAT he is.) I can say that uniformed Catholics (and by implication, all Christians) are doing a good thing by defending freedom against terrorists, but to call it an "act of Christian virtue" is a bit bewildering. Is this less messianic Jesus talk and more Constantinian? Is this a difference in kind or degree from what the Taliban are promised? I wish the Bishops and Mandela would have started their paper with the disproportionate amount of resources (is it 56%?) being used by one country with (is it now about 6%?) of world's population. The end of their statements at bottom of pg. 1 and top of pg. 2 should preface their discussion of war as lesser of two evils. Much of "just war" talk, with all its current and attendant subjectivity, legitimizes war as a primary good and blinds us to our "flawed policies and myopic lifestyles." Is there some way the Christian Church could address, without a shadow of a doubt, this issue? I was asked, soon after 9/11, to be a panelist sponsored

by the local Church of the Brethren. The topic was "What were historic peace churches to do in the face of terrorism?" I was asked to attend because I was thought to be in sympathy with nonviolence while a member of a "war" church!! That made me very uncomfortable, and honestly, somewhat tongue-tied. There is a lot more to be said about this.

3. I'm not sure we can reduce terrorism to psychopathology. To some degree, it is true. Is there some self-righteousness here? Does this fly in the face of the need to understand you pose on top of pg. 3? I have to stop; you can see how provocative your essay is. I relish the opportunity to chat in this way and would like it more in person.

4. I am judged by Niebuhr's critique. I am conflicted as to how agapaic love can be translated into agapaic justice and also international policy. RN doesn't finally satisfy me. Let's talk about that sometime. In correspondence with RN while I was doing my dissertation on MLK, he mentioned that King was not an absolutist in his pacifism, much less did King see himself trying to prove his purity (very important for RN), but he was very grateful for King's witness as a way of changing social injustice in the presence of a good bit of terror (he used "evil"). Admittedly, MLK and Gandhi had tappable consciences to deal with. I think the Muslim has such a conscience. By the way, I think Israel is hated also because it is an American colony and we've yet to reap that whirlwind. Gotta go Bill. Let's continue some time. It is a wonderful and powerful essay. Still conflicted and trying to make sense of it all.

Best, Ira

From Ira Zepp, December 5, 2001

Hi Bill,

It was getting late last night, so I decided to send off the response I was working on. More questions. These are not pro forma, but for a lot of reasons I'm working on these questions. A new Center on Nonviolence and Peace Education has opened here under the aegis of Common Ground and the reaction of the faculty has been interesting, if not a bit perplexing. So the questions last night and those today are not being asked in a vacuum.

1. Should Christians be at all sanctioning war as a "lesser" evil? I can see self-interested nation states and parties doing it. Is not "just war" for the Christian really an oxymoron? If Christians fight even in a "tragically necessary" war, does that make it "just" or "Christian" or a "virtuous act?" Is it possible to clarify or clean up our language when it comes to war? Or does our sinful condition move us in the direction of self-serving?

2. As theologians/church representatives, should our first reaction be to seek rationale for national or international conflict or should it be see the latter through the eyes of Isaiah, Jeremiah, Jesus? I am grappling with that prophetic eye and trying to appropriate their judgment on biblical and contemporary Israel, on Islam, Christianity and America and how that relates to the God (or the Devil) who acts in history. This means I need a reality check on my own biases, which people like you and other members of the Christian community can provide. I'd be happier going there first (to the prophet tradition and Jesus--not to what can appear as a

Constantinian privileged defense). Then, secondly, we can talk about the super-rich and vast amount of poverty around (to which you are acutely sensitive), and, then thirdly, attempt to justify our violent response. Does this order make any difference?

3. Re: psychopathology and terrorism. We had a speaker at WMC [Western Maryland College, now McDaniel College – ed.] a few weeks ago from the Counter-Intelligence Agency talking about our understanding of 9/11 and he tried to explain to us what produces contemporary terrorism. He included The Army of God, Church of the World Creator, The Aryan Nation, and other militia groups in this country (who feel our presently constituted government is illegitimate) and Hamas, Islamic Jihad, Hezbollah, the Taliban, etc. There were three major sources of terrorism according him: (a) God told me to do it. (This is very difficult to counter); (b) desperation, a feeling of nothing to lose, no future; and (c) this is the important variable today: the internet, instant communication, sophisticated technology. This triage concerned the officer very much; he warned us against labeling it "sickness." The 21st century will be a test of whether, and to what extent, we can try to understand this new "war." This next century will force us, as never before in history, to take a good look at ourselves. I cannot imagine that pain. What is/will the church do to help us with this?

4. Just yesterday I read Time, Dec.10, 2001. [Note that Time magazine is pre-dated by several days relative to its appearance on newsstands. – ed.] Lance Morrow on the last page has an essay in which he asks "Who's more arrogant?" He discusses very eloquently the "arrogance

of power" and the "arrogance of powerlessness" and in a way holds both western and Islamic feet to the fire. He suggests that the opposite of arrogance is not humility, but introspection. I recommend it to you. Morrow refers to Franklin Graham's words as "employing ayatullah vocabularies." He concludes: "The Muslim introspection must confront the failures of Islamic societies, political and economic and moral, and the evil, fascistic dreams that these societies sometimes export with vivid results. The Americans find themselves in the unaccustomed position of being the injured party. But eventually, when they have got a grip on the terrorist threat and return to calmer moments, they are going to have to give intelligent thought to turning their money and freedom to more decent, more responsible purposes. When they have put their flags away, Americans will have to ask if they want to go back to what they were on Sept. 10. They can do a lot better." I do wish I heard more of this from religious print and from Christian and Muslim pulpits. Is this too much to ask or too "unrealistic" to expect?

5. Wars, as you know, never produce peace. They produce cessation of conflict, which is, admittedly, no small matter. But to what extent is it possible for our domestic and international policy to reflect the notion that "ends are pre-existent in means" or that "means determines ends?" I'm not asking for utopia; I'm yearning for a more relative peace that more relatively peaceful means might produce. Maybe the best we can do is hope for a "cessation of conflict," or as you and Niebuhr might say "the containment of evil," but something in me resists that. King thought that agapaic love through

justice could bring a positive state of harmony. My "ambiguities, complexities and contradictions" as a virtual pacifist are clearly before me and I do not expect to get "out of the sinful contradictions of history," but, at the end of the day, I lean more toward Gandhi, MLK and others who had a more positive view of human nature that Niebuhr. THE 3000 CIVILIANS AND OTHER CASUALTIES OF 9/11 ARE VERY MUCH IN MY MIND'S EYE AS I WROTE LAST NIGHT AND TODAY AND I PRAY FOR THEM AND THEIR FAMILIES, FOR THIS COUNTRY AND FOR OUR CHURCH.

Thank you Bill for reading this. It allowed me to clarify some thoughts for myself. Further clarity would come if you responded in a critical fashion and I would be indebted to you.

Grace upon grace!!
Ira

From Bill Holmes, December 12, 2001

Dear friend Ira:

If you had only agreed or disagreed with me! Instead, you paid me the supreme compliment of taking my paper so seriously as to raise critical questions, which cause me to admit to the tentativeness of some of my own conclusions.

For instance, while I agree with you that there can never be a justification for nuclear war (I could never find a justification for the Vietnam or Gulf wars either), when I apply "just war" principles to our military response to 9-11, my paper jumps quickly to the conclusion that the principles for that war have been met, and then moves on. But, you rightfully challenge that conclusion as a premise for the rest of my argument.

I have to admit that I'm not nearly as convinced as I would like to be that our resort to the use of force in that war is a last resort, or that our bombing is proportionate. And, the one that bothers me the most, is what we're doing to noncombatants. Even though I trust the claims that we are attempting to bomb only military targets, and that we are making genuine efforts at humanitarian relief, and that we are liberating a whole country (especially its women) from a repressive regime, I'm still haunted by our "collateral damage" - especially when we mistakenly bomb a Red Cross installation twice, and hear reliable reports of hundreds of innocent causalities.

While admitting to these contradictions, and persisting in holding the non-pacifist position, I'm certain I cannot be excused from agonizing over the horrific consequences of my choice. That's why I've placed a picture from last Wednesday's Washington Post under the glass on my desk top. It's a picture of Noor Mohamed, age 10 (about the age of several of my grandchildren), who has lost both arms and is blind in both eyes as a result of a US bombing raid on his village.

Although I believe the terrorists themselves have some secondary responsibility for this and other atrocities, I can find no way to exonerate my own primary complicity in this abhorrent action. I know that if I'm going to claim the "realistic" point of view as a non-pacifist, I'm going to have to live with Noor Mohamed. He is only one of many. You mentioned at the beginning of your first email that you were "very conflicted" over your position as a "non-ideological, but relatively committed pacifist." Count me similarly inclined in my "Niebuhrian realism."

I also share your reservation about the Catholic Bishops' assurance to uniformed Catholics. To say that such soldiers are participating in an "act of Christian virtue" is one whale of a stretch, and not one that I could make either. I'm afraid the good bishops got carried away with their own rhetoric. At the same time, as I will argue a little later, I believe there are certain wars where legitimate goals and consequences are met, and where it is therefore appropriate to speak of a soldier's "Christian duty" - with all its ambiguities.

Your second email poses some tough questions. My attempted answers are more characterized by hesitancy than by certainty, but here goes:

1. "Should Christians be at all sanctioning of war as a "lesser evil?" I believe the decision-making process is always a matter of choosing between multiple "goods" and multiple "evils." In choosing a greater "good," lesser "goods" are neglected; in choosing a lesser "evil," greater "evils" are avoided. Since saying "yes" to one option usually means saying "no" to other options, it is humanly impossible to fulfill all "goods" or to avoid all "evils." Thus we can say with Paul, "The good that I would do I do not, and the evil I would not do I do." I think this is not only a statement about Paul's condition as a sinner who sometimes chooses evil, but also a statement about him as a creature who, for all of his good intentions, cannot avoid participating in evil.

2. "As theologians/church representatives..." This question seems to assume that seeing a historical event through the eyes of the prophetic tradition and Jesus means avoiding ambiguity, relativity and "lesser evils." I think that's idealistic and a-historical. I'm for turning to the prophets and Jesus first, just as long as we remember that even the birth of Jesus was the occasion for the "slaughter of the innocents." (This is probably not a good illustration of my point, since Jesus had no say in the matter, but it's a dramatic example of historic irony and the contradictory consequences of some historic events.)

3. Regarding psychopathology and terrorism. I'm a little puzzled by the speaker from the Counter-Intelligence Agency. How can he give the mindset, "God told me to do it." as one of the major sources of terrorism, and then warn against labeling terrorism as a "sickness?" I understand a psychopathology as a way of relating to reality through an illusion, a radically alien or unrealistic way of interpreting an event, usually accompanied by utter certainty. The more insecure a person is, the more that person is inclined to seek solace in illusions; and "God told me to do it." is a prime example of countering insecurity with a cosmic assurance. While I don't use the word "sickness" in my paper, I can't help but think there is some kind of psychopathology at work in the suicidal actions of terrorists - resulting in the deaths of thousands - who claim the approval of Allah.

4. I appreciated Lance Morrow's suggestion that the opposite of arrogance is not humility, but introspection; and that both Muslims and Americans have a lot to think about as a result of 9-11. I join you in the

wish that we heard more of this from religious print and from Christian and Muslim pulpits. To that end, it was encouraging to read yesterday editor John M. Buchanan's opening editorial in a recent issue of the Christian Century. It's entitled "Oil Dependents," and the gist in his observation is that we are willing to give our blood, just as long as we don't have to give up our profligate use of oil.[5]

5. I find quite provocative your statement that "means determine ends." I can't deny that in most instances its true. It is certainly the ultimate irony and futility of most wars. However, I have a hard time seeing it as necessarily true when force is used defensively and not aggressively. At an individual level, I don't see violence as more than a "transient end" in Bonhoeffer's decision to participate in the plot to assassinate Hitler. Surely peace and the relief of suffering would have been the more lasting ends of his use of force if the plot had succeeded. Similarly with the passengers who rushed the terrorists in the cockpit on the 9-11 flight that crashed in Pennsylvania. The end result of their use of force could have been lifesaving. To the extent that they altered the flight from striking DC, their act was valorous and heroic. At the level of the state, the best example is World War II. For all its tragedy and inhumanity at the time, the ultimate consequences of the conflict were humane and laudatory. (I exclude the dropping of the A-bomb, for which I think there was no sufficient justification.) In the end, through the Marshall plan and other efforts, the US helped former enemies to recover and rebuild. I'm just not sure that ends are always preexistent in means.

Also, while I hold Dr. King in the highest regard, I'm not as sure as he was that agapaic love through justice can always bring a positive state of harmony. The moment that love gets translated into justice, it takes on the characteristics of human finiteness: unevenness, relativity, and sometimes requiring the use of force. The "positive state of harmony" that it produces is partial, at best, and easily corrupted. I see Dr. King's statement as pertaining more to an end-of-time moment than a moment in historical time.

I know all this sounds terribly pessimistic and close to being hopeless. It seems to imply a kind of resignation that would settle easily for the status quo. One wonders where the motivation is to assume the prophet's mantle and cry "Thus sayeth the Lord." However, I am arguing that the Christian's primary motivation is not in the nurture of some idealism, but in a saving event of agape love. Our attempt to love as we've been loved is perpetually renewed in God's gift of grace, even though our efforts at justice continue to be flawed and accompanied by unintended consequences. This is both the irony and dignity of human history. We are Sisyphus, whose destiny is to roll a boulder to a summit only to watch it roll back down of its own weight. This need not be a cynical or pessimistic view of the human condition. Albert Camus argued that Sisyphus was neither hopeless nor dejected as he rolled his stone along. He understood the necessity and dignity of the struggle itself, even with its setback.

Ira, dear friend, forgive this lapse into homiletical flourish at the end. This response has turned out to be much too long and wordy. I have never been more honored than by the critical questions you raise about my paper. They have not only caused me to clarify my own position, but also to rethink some of my unexamined premises. I need you to keep me digging deeper, and to hold me accountable at every turn. As you know, such friendships are rare, and of inestimable value.

Grace upon grace to us both.
Bill

From Ira Zepp, December 12, 2001

Dear Bill,

Thanks so very much for your response. I can't tell you how grateful I am. I learned much more than you in the exchange; you have invited me to widen my King/Gandhi blinders. And you have learned your Reinhold Niebuhr lessons extremely well! That is at the bottom of the difference between us; of the two brothers, I'm more a Richard Niebuhr person. Reinhold's critique, like the Marxist critique, is indispensable as a critique, but it is difficult to make a platform from which to act or to plan the future. About which more later. I'm really looking for an alternative vocabulary to talk about war--beyond "just war" theory and even beyond King and Gandhi--which might lead to an alternative way of acting, of responding to violence. I hope it is not down the primrose path. (And as you've heard me say a few times, I'm looking for a re-freshing, re-newing, alternative spiritual language beyond my mixture of liberal/neo-orthodox/evangelical traditions. That's why I'm looking more closely at the mystics of all traditions. I'm really too old to be looking for alternatives, but that's where I am. I'd like to go through your responses in the order you list them.

1. I agree with you that decisions are incisions; they cut off other options, as you clearly state. Pacifists are not exempt from participating in evil; their decisions are not antiseptic, by any means, but while accepting the dialectical relation of good and evil and in the face of unclean choices, pacifists do their darndest to seek the greatest good and the least evil. And I'm sure you do as well. I'm sure you've seen the series of short articles in the Century, Nov. 14, 2001. I see some similarities between your position and J.B. Elshtain. The article toward which I leaned the most was Stasson's "just peacemaking" and the illustration of Eisenhower toward the end of his article, although I was not altogether happy with it either.

2. I don't want to put "historic irony" and "contradictory consequences" after the "but". I'd like the latter to come before the "but" and be qualified by the prophets and Jesus. This suggests an exegetical and homiletical issue. Given the unavoidable "ambiguity, relativity and lesser evils" of life, should Amos have said, "Let as much un-ambiguous justice as possible roll down like waters and relative righteousness flow like an ever flowing stream?" or "Hear the word of the Lord, which you are not expected to practice perfectly?" Or, notwithstanding the Jesus Seminar, Jesus saying, "Deny yourself as much as the contradictions of history allow you" or we preachers calling our people to be disciples, but with the limitations you face. Work with me, Bill. I want to stay here a while. I was wired by that old MYF slogan "Christ Above All," and that the earliest Christian confession

was not "Jesus, Soter," but" Jesus, Kurios." Talk about
incision!! You see, I'd rather proclaim the agapaic ideal,
as fragile as it is in practice, and know that the inevitable
fracturing of that ideal will find me adopting to some
degree a realistic position than start with "realism" and
know that its practice is also fractured and I end up
with a lower standard of agapaic justice. I've taught
King and Gandhi for the last 30 years and have been
greatly influenced by, to me, their well argued positions.
Gandhi, in commenting on the Sermon on the Mount,
which profoundly appealed to him and his Ahimsa
modality, once said (I think to C.F.Andrews in South
Africa) that Jesus, being the Son of God and presumably
knowing human nature, would not mock us by giving us
those hard sayings about "turning the other cheek," etc.
if we had not the capacity to practice them. I guess I'd
rather start with the ideals of Jesus, Gandhi, and King
and end with Niebuhr, than start with "realism" and
work in the ideals when I can. The priestly calibration
of the prophetic ideal will produce a more just society
depending on the elevation of that ideal. In other
words, the higher the bar of love, the more justice we
will realize. For example, Jesus' critique of lex talionis,
"eye for an eye," seems to trump any attempt at revenge
or retaliation. We now have values superior to the latter.
Gandhi and King, as I intimated earlier (and again with
personal and national consciences that could be appealed
to), took that method and turned SOCIETIES in a new
direction and concretely achieved measurable forms of
justice. Both Judaism and Islam, rooted in, held captive
by, the ethic of lex talionis are destroying each other in
the Middle East. I suppose nation states, including the
U.S., must act this way. Would there be more violence

if a "Gandhi" appeared on either side of West Bank? I sometimes think it (retaliatory ethics) is as much desert testosterone as something based on political theory. And then, Niebuhr may be right; societies/nations can't help wearing hubris on their sleeves. Parenthetically, I've been doing talks on Islam and Christianity almost every weekend these days and have tentatively concluded that a basic difference among the Abrahamic traditions is that Judaism and Islam spend a great deal of time studying and making sure the LAW, Torah and Shariah, is learned and practiced. Christianity seems to express a different emphasis with its centerpiece of LOVE. But in all fairness, in Judaism and Islam, love and mercy are in the Law (Psalm 1 and Sura 2:171), and in Christianity, law is found in love and grace (Romans 12). To me, that is a significant difference and one I want to continue to work on.

3. I totally (if that is Niebuhrianly possible) agree with your reflection here. You're right on with the pathology bit. I misrepresented the counter-intelligence guy. He was as hard on the "God told me" as you are. The METHOD used by the terrorists is sick, but the MESSAGE of the terrorists and many Islamists about the West is not sick.

4. YES

5. Means and ends. It was precisely used by King and Gandhi defensively. Their understanding of Agape and Ahimsa convinced them that loving/just means are more apt to produce loving/just ends than war trying to make peace or violence creating nonviolence. Could Niebuhr say "the MORE loving your means, the MORE loving your ends will be?" To the extent that racial integration

works today in the U.S. and that there are more humane relations among the races, it is due I feel, to the way King went about his reconciling. I'm glad you said the "best" example was WWII because the saturation bombing of Dresden and the A-bomb were far from appropriate means. I'd like to hear more from you on this. To me it is a fundamental issue. As you intimate, however, it may be more true in theory, than in practice.

Some additional thoughts:

1. I wonder how Sisyphus would have dealt with the stone if he felt embraced by grace.

2. Reinhold's theology is based on a graver view of human nature than I am, at this juncture, able to adopt. I appreciate the historical conditions of the early 20th century which helped him formulate that view. The Catholic tradition, along with Jewish, Islamic, and some small Protestant sects (those aberrant peace churches!), does not hold to such a negative, often debilitating view of human nature. Pacifists think of a relatively better human. In the small town of Darlington, MD, where I lived for the first 12 years of my life, there were two Quaker meetings and we knew those families well; they were a people apart. They always seemed to see war as a failure or sign of weakness.

3. But I hope I'm not turning into the bete noire of Reinhold, namely a liberal Protestant who thinks perfection is possible in this world and who adheres to some form of love monism of Jesus. I just believe that justice can not only be partially achieved in history, but more completely realized that we often believe. I can wait to the end time for its final completion.

4. I think we can fudge on too much grace and on too much realism. Adherents to both positions are often too dismissive of the other's contribution to the path of peace.

5. Let's not glory, and you so gracefully do not, in historic contradictions, inevitable ambiguities, etc. I'd like to be in the business of doing all I can, with all the will-power, grace, and dedication I have, to resolve them this side of heaven. Is that what discipleship is about? Thanks so much again, Bill. You've allowed me the chance to exchange, at a pretty deep level, some important issues and your response has been very helpful for romantic Ira. I'd give you a big hug if you were here.

From Bill Holmes, December 18, 2001

Dear Ira,

The Trollinger article[6] in the latest Christian Century was provocative and well balanced. It gave a helpful overview of shades of difference in the historic peace churches, as well as lifting up some voices of dissent to a pacifist response to 9-11.

As you would expect, I resonated most with Quakers Scott Simon and David Johns. It seems to me that these two men retain their pragmatic pacifism, while seriously asking, "What nonviolent options did we have to the 9-11 attacks?" Simon concludes, "...the U.S. has no sane alternative but to wage war, and wage it with unflinching resolution." Johns concludes, "The current military campaign, may not be perfect," but is something "we need to do" as one component of response to the threat of future terrorist attacks.

The quotation I had some questions about was from J. Denny Weaver, who contends, "It is unfair to assume that pacifists, who did not create the situation in the first place...can now be parachuted into the middle of the [crisis] with a ready-made solution." In fairness to Professor Weaver, it is likely that he has indicated in other writings what specific changes in U.S. foreign policy would likely have prevented 9-11. Otherwise, he would be in danger of assuming a dilettante position, and speaking to history from outside of history.

While Professor James Juhnke raises the same objection to folks who have "applied principles of violence and force that have not worked" now demanding solutions from the pacifists, he is able to match his objection with a concrete alternative - an international police force to bring terrorists to justice before an international court. While resorting to "the least force necessary," he is at least willing to be specific in offering a different strategy. Now, the only question is, "How much force would be necessary to succeed?" This is a question over which non-utopian pacifists might well disagree, but in any instance, force would be required. Or, as David Johns confesses, he cannot understand "what unilateral nonviolence would look like as American foreign policy."

Anyhow, the article certainly adds to our dialogue, and I appreciate your pointing it out.

Warmest regards,
Bill

From Ira Zepp, January 5, 2002

Hi Bill,

Thank you for your piece in The Connection.[7] Only you could articulate that position with such clarity and grace. I'm sure it will be well received and very helpful to many of us. It surely has been for me. I'm still concerned about a few things.

1. I mentioned earlier my misgivings concerning Niebuhr's assumptions about and understanding of human nature and history. I am haunted by his "simple Jesus love monism," and how difficult it is to translate that into public and international policy. What does discipleship and its cost mean here?

2. There is a Constantinian tinge about the piece which also bothers me. My understanding of the first couple of centuries of Christianity is that they were a (pretty effective) underground resistance movement and that being a soldier was virtually unheard of for those early generations. When Constantine gave the Church political sanction and we got in bed with the empire, it became necessary for Augustine to come up with the just war theory--the work of Natural Law. Otherwise, we might have all ended up as Mennonites, and other "peace churches."

3. It is painful to say this, but I have heard many preachers, including myself, who believe God acts in history, fulminate against godless nations and how God judges the latter through acts of history. I've even used "O Assyria, the rod of my anger and staff of my fury, against a godless (God bless Israel) nation I send you." But usually at a safe distance. What is God saying to

us through 9/11?   How does Niebuhr help us here?
Was he not an advisor to several presidents after 1932's
"Moral Man" and his "realism"?   Should we Christians
ever give power a pass?   Bill, I've benefited greatly from
your stimulating thoughts and the entire conversation.
Thanks again.   I'm looking forward to seeing you later in
the month at our meeting.   Have a great 2002.

Ira

From Ira Zepp, January 16, 2002

Hi Bill,

I'm sure you saw the piece in the Century yesterday
entitled "Caught in the Middle" by Michael Macdonald[8].
It reflects several themes in our conversation and I
find intriguing his "plague on both if no more of your
houses".   I like it because he raises more questions than
answers.   My question from reading him is "When do
the "truisms" or the "sloganeering" e.g. "violence in all
of its forms and expressions is contrary to God's purpose
for the world" and "love is stronger than all the forces of
evil" cease being "truisms" and "slogans" and / or how
do we go about implementing them and have them be
more visible as options for national and international
policy?   How best can we apply (admittedly a refraction)
Jesus in social and political life with as much of his ideals
in place as possible?   As I understand your concern, it
is not an either/or position, but some effective synthesis
or middle ground of "realism" and violence.   I might
be reading you wrong.   Am I?   This is why I need your
contribution for my deeper understanding and for our
conversation.   See you on Jan. 30.

Best, Ira.

From Bill Holmes, February 1, 2002

Dear Ira:

Please allow me a footnote to our dialogue, lest I misrepresent my mentor, Reinhold Niebuhr. At the end of our Wednesday session, you asked me if I thought Niebuhr believed that love (or peace) would eventually triumph in history. I think I answered "probably not." Riding home, I remembered a Niebuhr book in my library, entitled, "Beyond Tragedy." It's a series of essays on the question you posed. In the Preface he insists... "the centre, source and fulfillment of history lie beyond history." "It is the thesis of these essays that the Christian view of history is tragic insofar as it recognizes evil as an inevitable concomitant of even the highest spiritual enterprises. It is beyond tragedy insofar as it does not regard evil as inherent in existence itself but as finally under the dominion of a good God." I just wanted to be clear that I think Niebuhr's "pessimism" about human history is grounded in his understanding of our sinfulness, and that even that sin is finally overcome by God's grace and forgiveness.

While I'm writing, the other thing I did when I got home was read two articles that Jerry Weiss copied from "First Things" and brought to me. One was the Dec. 2001 article by The Editors, entitled "In A Time of War", the Feb. 2002 response by Stanley Hauerwas, and the Editor's response to Hauerwas. It's good to know that "our dialogue" is going on today in lots of places.[9]

But the one that really grabbed me, was the Feb. 2002 article, "The Continuing Irony of American History" by Wilfred M. Mc Clay. Have you read it? He says everything I've been trying to say - but so much better. And his knowledge of Niebuhr far exceeds my own. The only place I thought he jumped the track was at the top of p.25, in the left column. While I think he is right to warn that abortion, euthanasia, physician-assisted suicide and stem-cell experimentation can lead to a "medical and biotechnological degradation of human life," he stops being "Niebuhrian" by failing to also allow for the humanitarian values that can be derived from these breakthroughs as well. I believe Niebuhr would find the potential for both promise and tragedy in all of these examples - depending on how they were applied and for what reason.

Damn! This "footnote" has become an epistle! Sorry about its length. I'll close by saying I'm entirely converted to "First Things" and will be sending off my subscription pronto.

Stay well. You are a "means of grace" to more of us than you know - even when we disagree.

Bill

From Ira Zepp, February 1, 2002

Dear Bill,

Actually, the first thing I do with a new book is go to the footnotes or endnotes; they are often more interesting and insightful than the text. Thanks for yours! Re: Niebuhr's "fulfillment of history lies beyond history": I think MLK, Yoder, etc. might say "okay, but let's work as hard as we can to approximate in history what lies beyond it; live more eschatalogically, as they say."

Or to paraphrase Bonhoeffer, what is beyond tragedy

is also in the midst of tragedy, working its way through historical contradictions and ambiguity toward a fuller and richer humanity. I know how utterly foolish this sounds, given 9/11, and yet that foolishness may be wiser than we might think. I have subscribed to First Things since the mid-nineties and am fascinated by it--fascinated in the sense I mentioned the other day--I'm can't stay away from it and am repelled and disgusted by it at the same time. It is theologically sophisticated, well-written and rationally argued, sometimes too contentious (especially the Richard Neuhaus stuff), often maddening, but always provocative and beneficial for a romantic like me and that is why I like it. I always like to read the other side; it has been, in a "realistic way" my reality check. As I mentioned earlier, that Quaker community I knew as a child, Martin King, Gandhi, others in that tradition, and to some degree, now Hauerwaus[13] (although I disagree with a lot of other things he says) keep me what I think I've always been--a romantic (not a liberal!) out of which comes a hope, possibility, capacity for change, if not revolutions. Thank God, you're around to be my reality check. You are a Prince. Hang in there with the compassion that underpins the world.

Ira

Conclusion - Bill Holmes

Dear Ira,

Your generous invitation to write the conclusion to our email dialogue causes me to recall a note that Robert McAfee Brown once put at the top of a paper I wrote in a class at Union Theological Seminary. The paper was on John Wesley's concept of Christians' "going on to perfection." The gist of the paper was that Wesley never envisioned arriving at a perfect state in this world, but that Christians are under an imperative to strive and keep progressing. (A mandate reflected, I think, more in your point of view than mine.) While giving the paper a decent grade, Professor Brown wrote in the upper right hand corner, "I'm almost persuaded - but not quite!"

That's exactly how I feel about our dialogue. In many ways, I've moved closer to your perspective on the power and promise of non-violence. At the same time, in other ways, our dialogue has helped me clarify the reasons I cannot, in most instances, hold the pacifist position. "I'm almost persuaded - but not quite!"

The best quote of all, however, is from Reinhold Niebuhr. It represents an attitude that both of us try to practice, and that has made possible our lively, but mutually respectful exchange: "We must each be willing to see the truth in our opponent's error and the error in our own truth."[10] I'm grateful for the journey we have made together into that kind of effort.

Bill.

Notes:

1. Bill Holmes's position paper and the dialogue between Bill and Ira in this chapter were edited and are introduced by Charles Collyer.

2. Reinhold Niebuhr, 1940, quoted by E. J. Dionne, Jr., "Pacifists, Serious and Otherwise", Washington Post, October 29, 2001.

3. Report of U.S. Conference of Bishops, November 18, 2001.

4. Paul Hollander, "It's a Crime that Some Don't See this as Hate," Washington Post, October 21, 2001.

5. Editorial, "Oil Dependents", Christian Century, December 5, 2001.

6. William Vance Trollinger, Jr., "Nonviolent Voices", Christian Century, December 12, 2001.

7. An abridged version of Bill Holmes's position paper appeared in the January 2, 2002 UMConnection, a newspaper published bi-weekly by the Baltimore-Washington Conference of the United Methodist Church.

8. Michael McDonald, "Caught in the Middle," Christian Century, January 2, 2002.

9. First Things is a neo-conservative journal dedicated to the discussion of religion and public policy. Its editor is Richard John Neuhaus.

10. Reinhold Niebuhr, quoted by E. J. Dionne, Jr., Harvard Divinity School Bulletin, Winter, 2001-2002.

CHAPTER 9

Making Nonviolence Real

Charles E. Collyer

This chapter is concerned with realism: to what extent can nonviolence be made real in the world, and what does it look like when it is realized? We have presented many examples of nonviolence and approximations to nonviolence throughout the book. We hope that these examples and approximations have provided a glimpse of the inclusive or "big tent" conception of nonviolence that the authors have been developing. We hope that readers will see in these cases a kind of nonviolence that is robust and practical in everyday life.

However, there are two "reality issues" that we should discuss more fully and directly. One is a concern of scientists and policy makers: the issue of measurable outcomes. The other is a concern of professions charged with using force: the practicality of nonviolence in the face of violent threats.

MEASURABLE OUTCOMES

For the most part, when we have spoken of the "outcomes" of nonviolence in this book, we have meant changed attitudes toward other people and toward problem-solving. We have described these changes in words and stories rather than in statistical terms. For most social scientists, however, the measurability of outcomes is paramount. And in the disciplines concerned with human services and organizational development there is a branch of applied social science called program evaluation, which uses rigorous methodology to test for the existence of real effects of educational and other programs. This book is not a guide to quantitative research on the effects of nonviolence education. However, abundant research does exist, in fields such as psychology and education, and advanced study in nonviolence should include this literature. There are studies of the basic psychological processes that underlie aggressive and prosocial behavior. There are also applied "outcome studies" in which the impact of particular programs and interventions is documented. This research is rich in ideas related to nonviolence, and in evidence for the effectiveness of nonviolence education in its many forms. The research literature is much too vast to be reviewed in this book, but we would like to offer some entry points to this literature that we believe will make an immediate connection for the reader between our account of nonviolence and empirical research. Here are our suggestions:

A classic paper on children's imitation of aggressive behavior was published by Bandura, Ross, and Ross in 1961[1]. It demonstrated that children would copy the behavior and the words of an adult role model who was observed punching and yelling at an inflatable "Bobo doll". Young children were more likely to imitate if the role model was of their own gender, and boys were overall more aggressive than girls. The study was of theoretical importance because the researchers did not provide obvious rewards to the children for engaging in aggressive behavior. It led to a very large number of subsequent studies on various aspects of modeling and imitation, including research on the effects of watching violence on television. Bandura's famous Bobo doll study serves here as an example of important research on basic psychological processes relevant to violence and nonviolence.

A review article published by David Johnson and Roger Johnson in 1996 provides an example of scholarship focused on the effectiveness of programs to reduce violence. These authors reviewed the available literature on conflict resolution and peer mediation programs in schools. They concluded that, while the research was incomplete and problematic, several conclusions could be drawn:

a. Conflicts among students do occur frequently in schools (although the conflicts rarely result in serious injury).

b. Untrained students by and large use conflict strategies that create destructive outcomes by ignoring the importance of their ongoing relationships.

c. Conflict resolution and peer mediation programs do seem to be effective in teaching students integrative negotiation and mediation procedure.

d. After training, students tend to use these conflict strategies, which generally leads to constructive outcomes and…

e. Students' success in resolving their conflicts constructively tends to result in reducing the numbers of student-student conflicts referred to teachers and administrators, which, in turn, tends to reduce suspensions.[2]

Johnson and Johnson focused on conflict resolution and peer mediation programs, which we place under the "big tent" of nonviolence education programs. What about programs with other labels and vocabularies for putting what we call nonviolence into practice? Daniel Goleman, in his book *Emotional Intelligence,* provides an appendix called "Social and Emotional Learning: Results"[3]. In it he identifies several nonviolence-like programs which have had empirically validated outcomes, with literature references. The concerns addressed by these programs include child development, social development, social competence, awareness, problem-solving, and resolving conflict creatively. Again, we would see these as belonging under the big tent of nonviolence.

A study that directly examined the impact of Kingian Nonviolence training on the knowledge and attitudes of several groups who participated in two-day workshops, was done by Dr. Maram Hallak in 2000, and was mentioned at the end of Chapter 6 in this book. Dr. Hallak found changes in knowledge and attitudes that lasted for months after the workshops.

Are these programs an adequate sample? Are they simply a few "star" examples, selected for their success? Quite the contrary. We believe that these programs reflect a basic truth about teaching peaceful problem-solving: nonviolence works, and its effectiveness is demonstrated over and over again in the literature. One approach to demonstrating a program's effectiveness, using many studies from the research literature, is called meta-analysis. In this approach, a large number of studies on a topic are collected, and the results of the studies are pooled statistically to create a more powerful test of the effect's reality. Mark Lipsey and David Wilson wrote an article in 1993 titled "The efficacy of psychological, educational, and behavioral treatment: Confirmation from meta-analysis"[4]. Their paper actually contains the results of several meta-analyses on different kinds of treatments and programs, and using different kinds of outcome measures – a true tour de force of the meta-analysis approach. To cite only some of the results related to nonviolence training, the paper documents real effects in such categories as primary prevention education programs; social skills training; social learning treatment and diversion programs for juvenile delinquents; training in interpersonal cognitive problem solving skills for children; assertiveness training; and guidance and counseling programs. The magnitudes of the effects were measured, and in the categories just cited, the effects of the programs were found to be moderate in size – not huge, but not trivially small either. In other words, these are programs worth designing, investing in, and implementing; however, they should not be expected to produce dramatic change in every individual.

A great many other studies could be cited. The research supporting nonviolence education constitutes a strong empirical foundation for the development of programs aimed at teaching the skills of nonviolence. In a way, the social science research community has followed Gandhi's advice to experiment with nonviolence, to refine it and develop it further. Of course, we still need to translate what we know about nonviolence more fully into real life. And we need to keep studying and experimenting on new ways to create peace, and to train future generations to continue this work.

Nonviolence in the Face of Violent Threats
The terror attacks of September 11, 2001 set off a great many discussions about how people should respond to violence. The attacks were terrible in the extreme, and the deliberate killing of innocent people has been almost universally condemned – a tragic point of agreement throughout the months of public debate. There is also a general agreement – so general that it is rarely stated - that people want their leaders' responses to terrorism to make the situation better rather than worse. However, people have disagreed over whether particular responses, such as military counterattack in general, or particular forms of counterattack, are necessary or unnecessary, and whether they will actually make things better or worse.

Shortly after September 11, there were several sharp criticisms of "nonviolence" from commentators who took the position that the attacks provided a clear instance in which violent counterattack was justified, and where a nonviolent approach would obviously be inadequate. These commentators made the usual assumption that "nonviolence" means a passive acceptance of wrongdoing. Given that the acknowledged icons of nonviolence are Gandhi and King, who gave us powerful examples of non-cooperation with injustice, it is remarkable that this assumption persists. We trust that readers of this book now understand that real nonviolence vigorously seeks alternatives to both violence and to passive acquiescence in the face of threats, conflicts, and frustrating problems in general. As Walter Wink has said, and as Ira Zepp reiterated earlier in this book, it is a third path. It is actually a way of facing reality rather than avoiding it or lashing out.

The authors of this book share the disdain for passivity expressed by those commentators who, we feel mistakenly, set out after September 11 to protect the world from nonviolence. However, as teachers of active nonviolence, the post-September-11 debates have placed us under considerable pressure to explain our position. The pressure has come both from those whose readiness to resort to violence is quite high, and from others who simply hold the familiar misconceptions of what nonviolence is all about.

There is an approach to the justification of violence, called Just War Theory (JWT), which is often cited as setting limits on nonviolence by saying when war is justified. Let us offer a perspective on JWT from the viewpoint of nonviolence. Then we will consider how a commitment to nonviolence can be translated into several very difficult areas of application. Our aim is to show how nonviolence would look, and sometimes does look, in the real world.

JUST WAR THEORY: HALF A LOAF, AND YET SO FAR...

Just War Theory (JWT) proposes conditions under which a country is justified in going to war. Scaled down, it addresses the more general question of when a person is justified in using force to solve a problem.

JWT proposes that war is justified under the following conditions: it is fought by a legitimate authority; it is fought for a just cause; it is fought as a last resort after alternatives have been exhausted; and it is fought by ethical means. JWT also includes the traditional principles of discrimination and proportionality. Discrimination means that military personnel and resources, but not innocent civilians, may be targeted for attack. In warfare, imperfect discrimination is acknowledged to lead to some civilian casualties, a result euphemistically called collateral damage. Too much collateral damage may be considered "out of proportion" in any particular action, or for a war as a whole. So proportionality calls for the unwelcome judgment of how much damage is acceptable and how much is unacceptable. It can be seen that JWT offers a weighing of costs and benefits, both for war itself and for actions within a war.[5]

Another way to view JWT is that it is one approach to the setting of a threshold for violence. If a person or a country has a low threshold, they will fight their perceived adversary on very little provocation. If the threshold is higher, it means that they would need to be provoked more strongly, or that they would wait longer, before engaging in violence against their adversary. The existence of thresholds for violence, which vary from person to person, and which may even be expected to vary from time to time within one person, is not very controversial. It is in fact a realistic way to view violence. Ira Zepp conceded in the last chapter that he is aware of having a threshold, although for him it is very high ("on a scale of 1-10, I'd be something in the area of 9+".) Gandhi had a threshold, acknowledged in his example of the mad man running amok in a community, who would have to be stopped. Walter Wink admitted to being a violent man trying to get better, that is, to raise his threshold for violence.

Nonviolence aims to raise the threshold for violence, and hopefully raise it so high that violence never occurs. But it uses alternatives to violence, constructive problem-solving skills, and agape, both to raise the threshold and to fill the space then available for other kinds of action. Nonviolence goes beyond Just War Theory by proposing that, if we practice our skills of peacemaking and creative problem-solving, we may obviate the need for violence. It suggests that it is our responsibility as human beings to make sure that the conditions justifying war are never satisfied.

Is this idealistic? In one sense, yes. But, seen as a completely different attitude, nonviolence has very practical application in everyday affairs, from the personal to the global level. Nonviolence is about moving people from a position where their attention is focused on when they may have to fight, to a position where their attention is focused on adding more peaceful problem-solving to the world, so that there are fewer things to fight about. In this book we have described many of the skills of nonviolence that sometimes operate near the threshold where violence is about to begin. But more often we have been exploring ideas about how to work preventively, further below the threshold of violence, where "ordinary life" takes place.

Now, it is reasonable to assume that we will not always succeed in pushing the threshold of violence out of reach. Most advocates of nonviolence would accept the idea that, in extreme circumstances, force will become necessary to solve a problem. The September 11 example cited most frequently in this regard is Flight 93, the hijacked plane that crashed in the Pennsylvania countryside. Apparently the passengers on that plane took violent action against the hijackers, and in doing so prevented the destruction of government targets in Washington, DC. Would we have wanted those passengers, in the name of nonviolence, not to have risen up against the men who had taken control of the plane? No. In such circumstances, violent action to prevent even greater violence may be the only option available to people of good will. The problem is that people so often resort to violence while they still have other options available to them.

Advocates of nonviolence observe that Just War Theory is often used to rationalize violence. Paul Robinson's article, "Willing to kill but not to die", on the NATO bombing of Kosovo, is a powerful critique of the tendency of military powers to claim that the criteria of JWT have been satisfied, when in fact they have not, or when the question is at least still debatable. The implication is disturbing: rather than guarding against violence, JWT is available to the violence-prone, and to those who are trying to make up their minds, as an excuse for engaging in violence.

As we have noted previously, virtually every act of violence is justified in the mind of the violent actor as some kind of self-defense or legitimate response to threat, and therefore is felt to be necessary, at least for the moment. In nonviolence education, we are sometimes asked why we do not place more emphasis on proper ways to defend oneself. We try not to over-emphasize self-defense and other justifications, because people do not lack excuses for violence; quite the contrary – this is an area where human beings are already abundantly endowed. Highlighting self-defense keeps people thinking in old defensive, adversarial, reactive ways. Nonviolence represents a new way of thinking, not only about threat, but about all the times between threats.

We all do need alternative approaches for dealing with threat. Nonviolence offers a range of alternatives to the usual "fight or flight" dichotomy. This is not to say that nonviolence will always "work". But, tragically, for lack of a guarantee that it will work in the face of threat, nonviolence is seldom put to the test. Also, we easily forget that violence almost never "works"; in fact, violence should be seen as an indication of failure to solve problems successfully.

So what are some examples of nonviolent thinking in response to threat? Here are a few suggestions out of a vast repertoire of both commonplace and creative possibilities:

Consider the portion of the truth owned by your enemy. Consider the contribution that you may be making to the problem. Ask whether you have, and want, all the facts. Make an unexpected gesture that transforms the situation. Invite your enemy to tea. "Send in a thousand grandmothers"[6]. Refuse to insult and demean. Apologize. Talk, don't run away. Clearly state what you think is just, because maybe your enemy doesn't know. Grant amnesty. Provide constructive work. Offer a better deal. Ask your enemy to decide on a fair settlement, and then accept it. Build him or her a school or hospital. Resist denial; accept that these situations are really tough. Forgive. Ask for mediation. Send a gift. Recall when you were friends, and stop calling him or her evil. Remove a threat that you hold over him or her. Refuse to hate. Accept the decision of an arbitrator. Let it go. Go for life imprisonment rather than the death penalty. Support restorative justice over retribution. Say thank you. Regard violence as your real enemy. Be the one to stop the cycle of mutual humiliation, injury, and destruction. Find a way to be partners. Escape from the trap of enemy-thinking. Consider *agape*. Consider *ahimsa*.

These options and strategies are often uncomfortable, but they often "work". They have a much better, though less publicized, track record than violence. On the value of these nonviolent options, we are true believers. We feel that human beings too often fall into the trap of believing that the time for violence has come, when in fact there are still many realistic options available for solving problems peacefully and creatively, including, but not limited to, the ideas mentioned in the preceding paragraph. At the same time, we do not minimize the difficulty of taking the nonviolent approach. While better outcomes are more likely with nonviolence, the resistance most of us feel to reaching out in the spirit of nonviolence, can be paralyzing. Learning better how to overcome this paralysis is one of the major tasks ahead for nonviolence education.

On the question of whether violence is sometimes necessary or inevitable, on the other hand, we remain open-minded or agnostic. The logical necessity for violence has never been proven, but examples like Flight 93 suggest that there are times, with time short and an emergency at hand, when it is the only option. We accept that these times do come, and acknowledge that they would satisfy "just war" criteria. But we emphasize that such extreme cases are not very good guides to action most of the time.

More work has to be done to define the threshold for using force. JWT represents some of that work, and we grant that it has been well-intentioned. But: (1) JWT diverts attention and energy from "adding more peace" to the world; it focuses on the conditions under which we can permit ourselves to fail rather than the activities that would enable us to succeed. And (2) experience shows that JWT is used quite often to lower the threshold for going to war rather than to raise it; that is, it plays into our instinct to fight rather than holding us back from fighting.

The work of active nonviolence is not just to avoid violence, but to "add peace" - to promote work, fun, love, learning, and self-expression rather than violence. Making the world a more peaceful place is inherently worthwhile, and has the incidental side-effect of raising the threshold for violence.

Revisiting the Bill Holmes / Ira Zepp Dialogue

The exchange between Bill Holmes and Ira Zepp in Chapter 8 is instructive. Bill accepted the need for a version of Just War Theory, and so did not label himself an advocate of nonviolence. Ira Zepp expressed a preference for "aiming high", and not granting the inevitability of violence too soon. Both of these good men showed in their dialogue that they actually have a very high threshold for the use of force to solve problems, and care deeply about the need to avoid impulsive, vengeful, or casual uses of force. In this, and in their wonderful respect for each other, they seem alike although they used different terms to describe themselves. Their different emphases in talking about the implications of their high thresholds, give us a window into many of the issues, which are not at all new issues, raised by the watershed day of September 11. Perhaps the most pressing issue psychologically, is whether, having granted that a threshold for the use of force is realistic, we have in this moment arrived at that threshold.

Nonviolence and Law Enforcement

The acts called terrorism are crimes. Fighting crime is a job for legitimate law enforcement and a properly constituted judicial system. These are institutions charged with the responsibility to use force in the defense of society when necessary. What does law enforcement look like when it is informed and motivated by nonviolence?

A friend of ours, Captain Richard Tarlaian of the Providence RI Police Department, is a skilled nonviolence trainer with a strong commitment to good community policing. It is part of a police officer's job to talk with members of the public, to confront suspicious persons, to mediate disputes, to make arrests, and so on. In practice, officers have a certain latitude in performing these duties. They can be courteous and firm in their dealings with others, or demeaning and provocative. They can exhibit respectful behavior, which lays a foundation for future relationships, or they can sow the seeds of continuing hostility and resentment. When he is dealing with someone suspected of a crime, often someone distrustful of him and disrespectful toward police in general, Rich reminds himself to ask the excellent question: "Does this situation need another jerk?" And the answer, unsurprisingly, is "No." The question and the answer are a form of anger management. They are Rich's way of managing his own emotions and behavior in difficult, often angry situations, so that he does not magnify the problem at hand.

Another question Captain Tarlaian asks himself is "What if I need this guy to be my ally next week?" This question is a reminder that today's adversaries may become tomorrow's partners – an evolution of events that happens all the time. In the heat of a given moment, we may lose sight of another person's capacity to help us in the future. But nonviolence provides a framework within which it makes sense to remember truths that our emotions often hide from us. Richard Tarlaian's approach to policing is tough and realistic, but it is also informed by nonviolence.

Many people who identify themselves as peace advocates want nothing to do with the police. They identify the police as oppressors who maintain the power of the status quo. The authors' brand of progressivism does not subscribe to this kind of rhetoric. It is certainly true that police departments are the source of many horror stories regarding the use of violence and intimidation against less powerful people. These stories ought to be instructive examples of what to avoid. But we have seen many good police officers who, by nurturing young people toward more constructive lives, and in many other ways, contribute tangibly to addressing society's problems.

Consideration of policing and law enforcement invites an important question: What is the difference between force and violence? That is, are there some uses of force that lie below the threshold of violence? If so, then we want the legitimate use of force to be in a police officer's job description, but we would still want to keep violence out.

The difference between just force and unjust violence can be illuminated by our examination of nonviolence. Martin Luther King offered a simple and compelling definition of justice as that which uplifts the human personality, and of injustice as that which degrades it. With the job description of police officers, or with any other human relationship in need of definition, we can make good use of King's approach. Many effective police officers value human personality, respect their fellow citizens, and look beyond the present moment toward the needs of tomorrow when dealing with difficult characters. They are in line with King's definition of justice, and with the practical ideal of nonviolence. It is not easy, but that can also be said of nonviolence in general.

In many jurisdictions today, the official professional training in the police academy at least acknowledges the values of respect and human rights. These values are also strengthened by the personal beliefs of many individual officers. A continuing task for police training will be to present these values within a larger framework that motivates and educates all officers to perform their duties as nonviolently as possible.

As a society, we have not outgrown our need for the police. The question is what kind of policing we will demand and support.

Nonviolence in Corrections

Prisons embody society's overriding desire to avoid the problems of crime and violence. The goal of *solving* these problems is secondary to this desire for avoidance. Offenders are sent away because they have offended us - made us angry, fearful, and vengeful. We think we will teach them a lesson. Of course, they very often learn other lessons than we intended while they are incarcerated. Once they are behind bars, we prefer to neglect them rather than invest in turning them around (although it must be said that many professionals in the field of corrections would have it otherwise). In other words, we leave them to spend their time with and be further educated by precisely the people we most fear and despise. This approach to "corrections" exacerbates, rather than corrects, violent criminal behavior. Society has chosen a hostile, adversarial approach, which guarantees that it will continue to be plagued by violence. What could be further from the spirit of nonviolence?

There are many organizations working to reform society's approach to the organizational aspects of prisons and to corrections philosophy in general. We cannot review all these efforts here, but we applaud them. Corrections is an important arena in which to pursue our best practices of promoting personal change. Perhaps surprisingly to some, nonviolence programs and other forms of educational programming are very welcome in many prisons, and receive a positive response from a large proportion of administrators, staff, and inmates.

Nonviolence in the Military

If we can conceptualize nonviolent law enforcement, or an approximation to it, and moves toward nonviolence even in prisons, what about the military? A nonviolent military at first seems to be the ultimate contradiction in terms. Yet, if we are to consider extending nonviolence into the most threatening real situations, and into the work of people charged with wielding a truly awesome potential for violence, this is exactly what we must consider.

First, it may be helpful to reconceptualize military action in terms of law enforcement rather than war. Again, if nonviolence can influence the use of force in policing, the same principles should carry over to national defense. One can discern moves in this direction over the past century, at least in the rhetoric used to describe and justify the use of military force. The Korean War was called a police action. The United States is said to be cast in the role of the world's policeman. And so on. However, a serious reframing of the role of the military as enforcing the law may be helpful. For one thing, the principle of proportionality seems to be observed more carefully in the work of most law enforcement agencies than in the work of war. "Collateral damage" is not accepted and swept under the rug in police work as it often is in war. Strategies for minimizing violence and destruction are more central to policing, which takes place in the community, than in war, which is intentionally carried to the enemy's community. So a shift away from large-scale violence toward a more measured use of force might begin with thinking of the military's job in terms of law enforcement, and imagining what that would look like.

Nonviolence has its own forms of fighting, and we have discussed some of them in this book. The activist Bernard LaFayette Jr. embraces the metaphor of nonviolent warriors, trained to fight injustice. The Montgomery bus boycott has been described as a nonviolent war, and its veterans, when they gather, have all the *esprit de corps* and recapture all the camaraderie of any veterans' organization. Today there are Peace Brigade groups, which interpose themselves in zones of conflict, and there are proposals to create national or international military units to do the same. The military do not always need to go to war, or prepare for war. They can also go to keep peace, and work to prevent war using the larger repertoire of skills suggested by nonviolence.

Military force is an instrument of a nation's foreign policy, and so we should also note the need for envisioning nonviolence in this arena. Sadly, countries often do not practice the same values internationally that they espouse at home. A nation may stand for democracy, freedom, and self-determination, and yet its foreign policy may have the effect of denying these rights to other people through interference in elections, support for ruthless dictators, and other forms of diplomatic violence. A good start toward a nonviolent foreign policy for the United States would be to consistently promote its own values, rather than their opposites, overseas. If this were done, it is more likely that a proper role for the U.S. military in this dangerous world could be agreed upon.

Large-Scale Nonviolence in History

It is probably true, as Walter Wink has said, that the world is not ready for real nonviolence. However, it must be ready for whatever it _is_ ready for – for the steps that can be taken in this generation to move us toward nonviolence. We need to think of nonviolence in broad, relative, and practical terms if we are to take these steps, because they will not necessarily look like "pure" nonviolence.

Actually, history provides quite a few examples of large-scale nonviolence – democracy, laws, courts, human service programs, education. Over time, the impact of these forms of nonviolent problem-solving has tended to increase. For example, the voting franchise in the United States has expanded steadily from a few white men to former slaves, to women, and finally to 18-year-olds. Higher education was once the privilege of only a few, but now is the expectation of about half the population in North America. In just the past generation, the shelters for victims of domestic abuse provide a wonderful example of a nonviolent response to a problem of violence in society. The shelters are not places of pure pacifism; they are very hands-on, nuts-and-bolts, practical problem-solving places. A generation ago, they hardly existed.

Viewed in this way, there has been progress toward a more nonviolent world. However, the word nonviolence is usually not associated with these examples. We wonder why, and invite you to re-examine what nonviolence really means, with these examples in mind.

In the Final Analysis

If we are successful in building a peaceful world – a world of work and love and fun and fellowship and fulfilling self-expression - it will not feel like "violence prevention", but incidentally it will be so. This feature of nonviolence, that when it is successful it makes the thought of violence recede and the word nonviolence itself seem less relevant because of its etymology, is ironic. It is as if during every period of daylight we forgot about the phenomenon of darkness. When violence is out of sight, it is kept out of mind by powerful forces of avoidance and denial. New ways of thinking are necessary, both to build a peaceful world, and to hold forgetting at bay in the process.

We have a new paradigm to teach, a third path to replace the old dichotomy of complacency and violence. This third path is, as Gandhi said, as old as the hills. It continues to be rediscovered century after century, with new refinements and examples added each time. From the ahimsa of Buddha to the agape of Jesus, to the moral outrage of Thoreau and Tolstoy against unjust state power, to the syntheses of Mahatma Gandhi and Martin Luther King Jr. in the twentieth century, to the work of Danilo Dolci in Sicily, of Aung San Suu Kyi in Myanmar (Burma), of the Truth and Reconciliation

Commission in South Africa, of Mairead Corrigan Maguire in Northern Ireland, and many others today, nonviolence has grown new insights and new applications.

It is time to see nonviolence as a paradigm for everyday life, and not simply as a courageous and counterintuitive approach that we are driven back toward by new crises. Our challenge in the years ahead will be to see in nonviolence a basic ethical and practical foundation for all of life, not just for the one percent in which we feel threatened. The task of extending nonviolence into the other ninety-nine percent is a worthy one for of all of us.

Notes:

1. Bandura, A., Ross, D., and Ross, S. A. (1961) Transmission of aggression through imitation of aggressive models. *Journal of Abnormal and Social Psychology*, 63, 575-582.

2. Johnson, D. W. and Johnson, R. T. Conflict resolution and peer mediation programs in elementary and secondary schools: A review of the research. *Review of Educational Research*, Winter 1996, 66, No. 4, 459-506.

3. Goleman, D. *Emotional Intelligence: Why it can Matter More than IQ.* New York: Bantam, 1995.

4. Lipsey, M. W. and Wilson, D. B. (1993). The efficacy of psychological, educational, and behavioral treatment: Confirmation from meta-analysis. *American Psychologist*, 48, 1181-1209.

5. The description of Just War Theory paraphrases Paul Robinson's in his article titled "Ready to kill but not to die: NATO strategy in Kosovo", *International Journal* , Autumn 1999.

6. "Send in a thousand grandmothers" is the first line of the song 1000 Grandmothers, by singer and activist Holly Near.

Suggested Reading

Ackerman, P. and Duvall, J. A Force More Powerful: A Century of Nonviolent Conflict, New York: St. Martin's Press, 2000.

Baillie, Gil, Violence Unveiled: Humanity at the Crossroads, New York: Crossroad Publishing, 1997.

Barash, D. P. (ed.), Approaches to Peace: A Reader in Peace Studies. New York: Oxford University Press, 2000.

Barash, D. P. and Webel, Charles P., Peace and Conflict Studies. Thousand Oaks CA: Sage Publications, 2002.

Beck, A. Prisoners of Hate: The Cognitive Basis of Anger, Hostility, and Violence, New York: HarperCollins, 1999.

Bondurant, Joan V., The Conquest of Violence: The Gandhian Philosophy of Conflict, Berkeley: University of California Press, 1967.

Brown, Judith M., Gandhi: Prisoner of Hope, New Haven: Yale University Press, 1989.

Bullard, S. Teaching Tolerance: Raising Open-Minded, Empathetic Children, New York: Doubleday, 1996.

Christie, Daniel J., Wagner, Richard V., Winter, Deborah DuNann, Peace, Conflict, and Violence: Peace Psychology for the 21st Century, Upper Saddle River, NJ, Prentice Hall, 2001.

Dear, John, Living the Peace: Spirituality of Contemplation and Action, NY: Doubleday, 2001.

Diamond, L., The Peace Book, 3rd ed. Bristol, VT: The Peace Company, 2001.

Easwaran, Eknath, Nonviolent Soldier of Islam, Badshah Khan, A Man to Match His Mountains, Tomales, CA: Nigiri Press, 1999.

Ferguson, John, War and Peace in World Religions, NY: Oxford University Press, 1978.

_____, The Politics of Love: The New Testament and Nonviolent Resistance, Nyack, NY: Fellowship Publications, 1979.

Gandhi, M. K., Nonviolent Resistance, NY: Schocken Books, 1968.

_____, The Law of Love, Bombay: Bharatiya Vidya Bhavan, 1962.

_____, An Autobiography: The Story of My Experiments with Truth, Boston: Beacon Press, 1957/1993.

Garrow, David, Bearing the Cross: Martin Luther King, Jr., and the Southern Christian Leadership Conference, NY: William, Morrow and Company, Inc., 1986.

Gilligan, J., Violence: Reflections on a National Epidemic, New York: Random House, 1996.

Harak, G. Simon, Nonviolence for the Third Millennium,

Macon, GA: Macon University Press, 2000.

Halberstam, D. The Children, New York: Fawcett, 1998.

Hanh, Thich Nhat, Touching Peace: Practicing the Art of Mindful Living. Berkeley: Parallax Press, 1992.

Holmes, R. L. and Gan, B. L. Nonviolence in Theory and Practice, 2nd ed. Long Grove IL: Waveland Press, 2005.

King, Martin Luther, Jr., Stride Toward Freedom: The Montgomery Story, NY: Harper and Row Publishers, 1958.

_____, Strength to Love, Philadelphia: Fortress Press, 1981.

LaFayette, B., Jr., and Jehnsen, D. C., The Leaders' Manual: A Structured Guide and Introduction to Kingian Nonviolence, The Philosophy and Methodology, Galena OH: Institute for Human Rights and Responsibilities, 1995.

Lantieri, L. and Patti, J. Waging Peace in Our Schools, Boston: Beacon Press, 1996.

Lefebvre, Leo, D., Revelation, The Religions and Violence, Maryknoll, NY: Orbis Books, 2000.

Lewis, J. Walking With the Wind: A Memoir of the Movement, New York: Simon and Schuster, 1998.

Macgregor, G.H.C., The New Testament Basis of Pacifism and The Relevance of an Impossible Ideal: Answers to Reinhold Niebuhr, Nyack, NY: Fellowship Publications, 1954.

MacNair, R. M., The Psychology of Peace. Westport, CT: Praeger, 2003.

Maguire, M. C. The Vision of Peace, Maryknoll NY: Orbis Books, 1999.

May, Rollo, Power and Innocence: Search for the Sources of Violence, NY: Delta Publications Co., 1972.

McCarthy, C. All of One Peace: Essays on Nonviolence, New Brunswick NJ: Rutgers University Press, 1994.

Nair, K. A Higher Standard of Leadership: Lessons from the Life of Gandhi, San Francisco: Berrett-Koehler Publishers, 1997.

Nygren, Anders, Agape and Eros, Translated by Philip Watson, NY: Harper and Row, 1969.

Paige, G. D., Nonkilling Global Political Science. Xlibris Corporation: www.Xlibris.com, 2002.

Polner, Murray, Goodman, Naomi, Editors, The Challenge of Shalom: The Jewish Tradition of Peace and Justice: Philadelphia: New Society Publishers, 1994.

Sharp, G., Waging Nonviolent Struggle. Boston: Porter Sargent Publishers, 2005.

Smith, K. L. and Zepp, I. G. Jr. Search for the Beloved Community: The Thinking of Martin Luther King Jr., Valley Forge: Judson Press, 1974/1998.

Thoreau, H. D. Civil Disobedience. In Bode, C., Editor, The Portable Thoreau, New York: Penguin, 1975.

Tolstoy, L. The Kingdom of God is Within You: Christianity Not as a Mystic Religion but as a New Theory of Life, translated by Constance Garnett. Lincoln, Nebraska: University of Nebraska Press, 1984.

Ury, W. Getting to Peace: Transforming Conflict at Home, at Work, and in the World, New York: Viking, 1999.

Volf, Miroslav, Exclusion and Embrace: A Theological Exploration of Identity, Otherness, and Reconciliation, Nashville: Abingdon, 1996.

Walzer, M., Just and Unjust Wars, 3rd ed. New York: Basic Books, 1999.

Washington, J. M., Editor, A Testament of Hope: The Essential Writings and Speeches of Martin Luther King, Jr., San Francisco: HarperCollins, 1986.

Wink, Walter, Engaging the Powers: Discernment and Resistance in a World of Domination, Minneapolis: Fortress Press, 1992.

Yoder, Peter, B., Shalom: The Bible's Word for Salvation, Justice, and Peace, Nappance, Indiana: Evangel Publishing House, 1987.

ISBN 142510425-8

9 781425 104252